FY 2013 Annual Performance Report
FY 2015 Annual Performance Plan

U.S. Department of Housing and Urban Development

July 2014

About This Report

This Fiscal Year (FY) 2013 Annual Performance Report (APR) and FY 2015 Annual Performance Plan (APP) for the U.S. Department of Housing and Urban Development (HUD) provides detailed performance-related information to the President, the Congress, and the American people. The report allows readers to assess HUD's FY 2013 performance, revisions to FY 2014 goals, and plans for FY 2015 relative to its mission and stewardship of public resources. This report consists of several important sections:

Agency and Mission

This section contains HUD's mission statements, its vision, organizational structure, and scope of responsibilities, as well as an introductory message from the HUD Secretary, Shaun Donovan, in which he highlights key FY 2013 program accomplishments and policy priorities going forward.

Strategic Goals and Strategic Objectives

This section contains HUD's strategic framework, as established in the new _HUD Strategic Plan FY 2014-2018_. It is comprised of four overarching strategic goals and 12 strategic objectives which help frame HUD's discussion of its performance targets and associated priorities. The majority of this APP-APR is organized by strategic objective. Strategic objectives are intended to reflect the outcome or management impact an agency is trying to achieve. Each objective will be tracked annually through a specific set of performance indicators. In addition, HUD's strategic framework contains eight management objectives that are intended to improve departmental operations.

Figure 1 This sample strategic flow demonstrates how the strategic goals, strategic objectives, performance goals, and Agency Priority Goals should cascade from the Department's mission.

Please note that Agency Priority Goals (or APGs) are denoted by a ✪ throughout this document. Each agency is responsible for identifying a limited number of performance goals that are high priorities over a two-year period. These APGs support improvements in near-term outcomes, customer service, or efficiencies, and advance progress toward longer-term, outcome-focused strategic goals and objectives in an agency's Strategic Plan. Thus, while strategic objectives are evaluated annually and focus on longer-term performance goals, Agency Priority Goals are evaluated quarterly and focus on near-term results.

For each strategic goal, we have included its associated strategic objectives, an overview of the problem(s) HUD is attempting to address through these objectives, strategies for achieving the objectives, goal leaders, major milestones, and performance indicators to track our progress. HUD's APGs were established in FY 2012 to cover a two-year performance period (FY 2012-2013). Thus, in this consolidated FY 2013 APR and FY 2015 APP, we present to readers a synopsis of both final outcomes on the FY 2012-2013 APGs, and plans and targets for the FY 2014-2105 APGs.

For most metrics, HUD has committed targets for FY14 and FY15 which will enable us to track our performance in the next two years. For some metrics, we are still gathering data to establish baselines and preparing to set targets in future years. These metrics are indicated with the phrases "Establish Baseline" and "Target TBD" in the relevant tables. A third category of metrics, marked as "Tracking Only", provide information about program operations or external conditions but will not have targets. For these metrics, targets would be difficult to establish, would not provide meaningful indications of agency performance expectations, and/or could create unintended incentives for program staff and our partners.

Additional Information

This final section includes required supporting information, including a description of HUD's data-driven management review process, a summary of both completed and upcoming evaluations and research to inform progress on our strategic goals, and a section on data validation and verification.

Table of Contents

Section 1

Agency and Mission

Introductory Message from the Secretary

It is a pleasure to present the U.S. Department of Housing and Urban Development's Fiscal Year 2013 Annual Performance Report (APR) and Fiscal Year 2015 Annual Performance Plan (APP).

It has been another year of progress at HUD. As this report details, our work to expand opportunities for families and communities is making a profound difference on the ground. In Fiscal Year 2013, we assisted **493,985** families at risk of foreclosure. Working with our federal partners, through the *Opening Doors* plan, the number of persons experiencing homelessness dropped 4 percent since 2012.

In total, HUD's efforts has helped generate new hope and progress in communities across the country—critically important work as our nation fights its way back from an historic economic crisis. As a result, the housing market has made a comeback with sales, construction starts, home equity and other important measures all trending in the right direction. However, our work is not finished which is why this FY 2015 Annual Performance Plan outlines ambitious goals that will build on the gains already made.

Among our priorities, we will continue to strengthen the Federal Housing Administration to preserve its decades-long mission of providing access to credit for families—of all income levels—who are ready to buy. We will also continue to push for housing finance reform to strengthen the housing market, give responsible households a fair chance to purchase a home and ensure a crisis of this magnitude never happens again.

To give more families access to quality housing options, HUD is working with partners to preserve and produce affordable units. With our clean energy initiatives, we are also bringing more economic and environmental benefits to communities. Finally, through efforts like Choice Neighborhoods and Promise Zones, in partnership with leaders at the federal and local levels, we are using a comprehensive approach to revitalize areas that have been in distress for far too long.

HUD has put forth these and the other initiatives outlined in this document with one goal in mind: building ladders of opportunity that reach all Americans. From children born into poverty, to veterans sleeping on the street, to seniors struggling to retire with comfort and dignity, HUD is committed to giving every person a fair chance to lift themselves up and better their lives. Ambitious goals? Yes, but we will not rest until we achieve them. We look forward to working with a wide-variety of partners on these efforts. Together, we can make this opportunity agenda a reality for generations to come.

Lastly, the 2015 Cuts, Consolidations, and Savings (CCS) volume of the President's Budget identifies lower-priority program activities, where applicable, as required under the GPRA Modernization Act, 31 U.S.C. 1115(b)(10). The public can access the volume at: http://www.whitehouse.gov/omb/budget

Shaun Donovan
Secretary

HUD's mission is to create strong, sustainable, inclusive communities and quality, affordable homes for all.

Our vision is to improve lives and strengthen communities to deliver on America's dreams. Therefore, we pledge—

▶ For our Residents: We will improve lives by creating affordable homes in safe, healthy communities of opportunity, and by protecting the rights and affirming the values of a diverse society.

▶ For our Partners: We will be a flexible, reliable problem solver and source of innovation.

▶ For our Employees: We will be a great place to work, where employees are valued, mission driven, results oriented, innovative, and collaborative.

▶ For the Public: We will be a good neighbor, building inclusive and sustainable communities that create value and investing public money responsibly to deliver results that matter.

Introduction

HUD requested for Fiscal Year 2015 $46.7 billion in gross discretionary budget authority. Eighty five percent of this amount is needed solely to renew rental assistance to almost 5 million residents of HUD-subsidized housing, including 2.16 million households assisted with Housing Choice Vouchers, and to renew existing HUD grants to homeless assistance programs. Detailed data on over 4.3 million tenants reveals that: 56 percent are elderly or disabled, 75 percent are extremely low-income (below 30 percent of area median income) and an additional 20 percent are very low-income (below 50 percent of area median income). The Department's programs are critical to addressing the structural gap between household incomes and housing prices and the persistent unaffordability of housing. HUD plays an important role in making housing affordable through its investments in rental vouchers, public and assisted housing, and HUD-funded efforts led by states and localities. These efforts recognize that ensuring a stable supply of affordable housing in safe and quality communities enables low-income families and individuals to live healthy and productive lives. HUD is also a vehicle for advancing sustainable and inclusive growth patterns, communities of choice, energy efficiency, and community and economic development, and enforcing fair housing, strengthening the nation's mortgage market, as well as reducing homelessness.

- ▶ **Learn more about HUD's major organizational units and program offices.**
- ▶ **Learn more about HUD's regions and field offices.**

In carrying out its work on each of its strategic goals, HUD is committed to the following **core values**:

- ▶ **Accountability:** We individually and collectively take responsibility for our performance and conduct.

- ▶ **Efficiency and Effectiveness:** We will maximize our resources and efforts to continually improve the efficiency and effectiveness of our individual and collective performance. We strive for simplicity in our lines of authority and clarity in our lines of communication and to eliminate the red tape of bureaucracy. We support a productive work environment that balances high performance with the need for healthy personal and community life.

- ▶ **Fairness and Respect:** We value each other, demonstrate compassion for those we serve, and treat others the way we would like to be treated. In respecting others, we conduct our work and administer our programs with fairness and justice, and with a commitment to civil rights, inclusion, and diversity.

- ▶ **Integrity:** We approach each other, our stakeholders, and our work with honesty and the highest ethical standards

- ▶ **Teamwork:** We work together in a spirit of camaraderie, trust, and collaboration. We believe that by contributing our individual strengths we can accomplish more together than separately. We are open-minded, ready to adapt, and willing to embrace innovation and creativity when confronting challenges in our workplace.

HUD's Organization and Reporting Structure

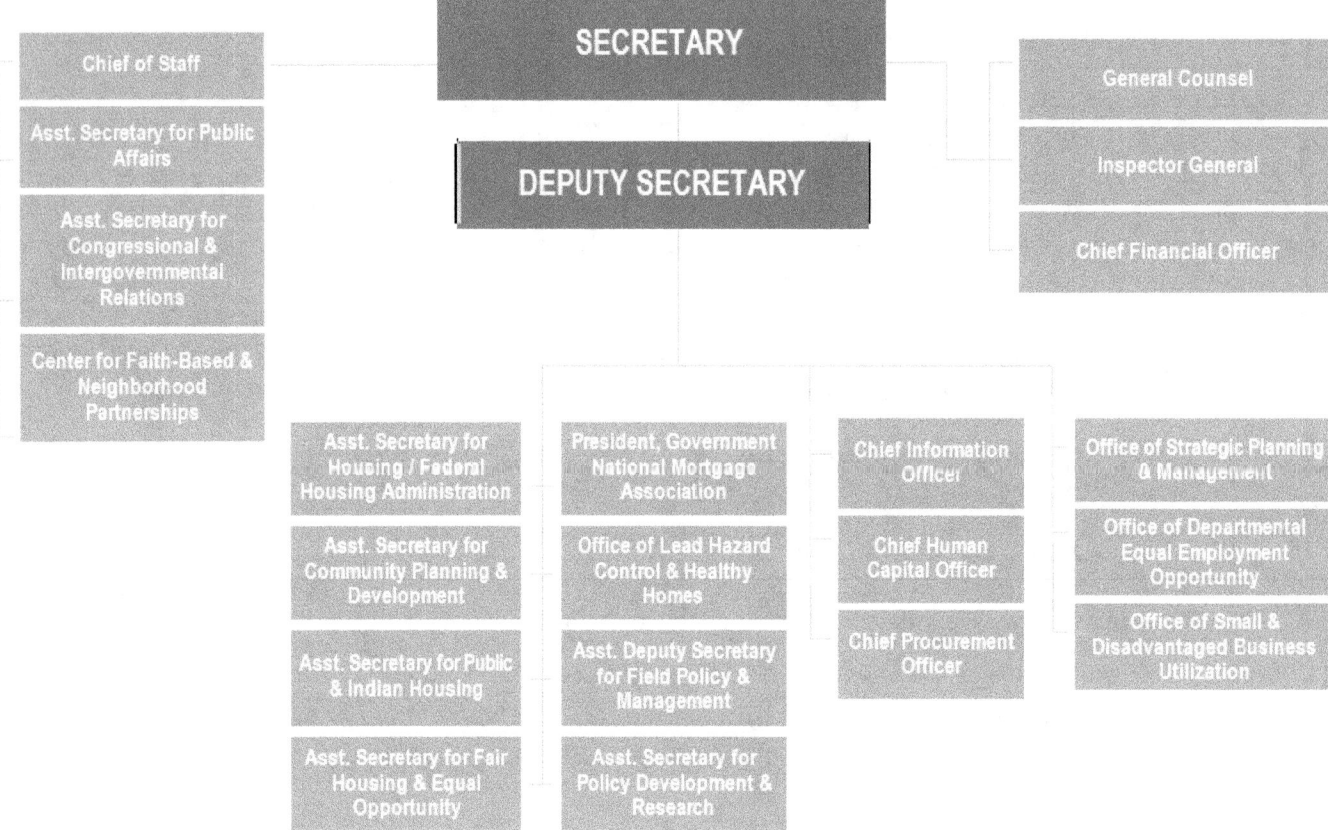

" I'M NOT INTERESTED IN NUMBERS AND DATA FOR THEIR OWN
SAKE—BUT RATHER FOR WHAT THEY CAN TELL US. I
BELIEVE THERE IS REAL VALUE IN SETTING CLEAR,
QUANTIFIABLE GOALS AND MANAGING PROGRESS AGAINST
THEM. TOO OFTEN IN GOVERNMENT, WE'RE NOT EVEN SURE
WHAT SUCCESS LOOKS LIKE. SETTING THESE KINDS OF
GOALS NOT ONLY CREATES RALLYING POINTS FOR
GOVERNMENT AGENCIES—COLLECTIVELY THEY ALSO
CREATE A VISION FOR WHAT SUCCESS LOOKS LIKE AND
WHAT THE RESPONSIBLE STEWARDSHIP OF TAXPAYER
DOLLARS OUGHT TO LOOK LIKE. "

—Secretary Shaun Donovan

FY 2013 BY THE NUMBERS

493,585 homeowners at risk of foreclosure who were assisted through HUD's early delinquency or loss mitigation programs

92% percent of homeowners who were then able to avoid re-defaulting on their mortgage payments, in the 6 months after receiving loss mitigation assistance

74% percent of "neighborhood investment clusters" (receiving funds from HUD's Neighborhood Stabilization Program) that showed lower vacancy rates after investment, compared to similar neighborhoods that did not receive this HUD investment

35,534 increase in occupied affordable rental housing units, on top of the approximately 5.4 million units of HUD affordable rental housing occupied at the end of 2012

14,666 veterans who were homeless or at risk of homelessness who were provided with HUD-VA Supportive Housing

4% estimated decline in overall homelessness between 2011 and 2013, despite extremely challenging economic climate

14% estimated decline in homelessness among veterans between 2011 and 2013

75,951 new or retrofitted cost-effective housing units that were healthier, more energy-efficient, or met green building standards, with the support of HUD investments

Section 2

Strategic Goals &
Strategic Objectives

HUD's FY 2014 – 2018 Strategic Framework

Mission: Create strong, sustainable, inclusive communities and quality, affordable homes for all.

Strategic Goal 1	Strategic Goal 2	Strategic Goal 3	Strategic Goal 4
Strengthen the Nation's Housing Market to Bolster the Economy and Protect Consumers	Meet the Need for Quality Affordable Rental Homes	Use Housing as a Platform to Improve Quality of Life	Build Strong, Resilient, and Inclusive Communities

Strategic Objectives

Strategic Objective 1A Establish a sustainable housing finance system that provides support during market disruptions, with a properly defined role for the U.S. Government.	**Strategic Objective 2A** Ensure sustainable investments in affordable rental housing.	**Strategic Objective 3A** End homelessness for Veterans, people experiencing chronic homelessness, families, youth and children.	**Strategic Objective 4A** Reduce housing discrimination, affirmatively further fair housing through HUD programs, and promote diverse, inclusive communities.
Strategic Objective 1B Ensure equal access to sustainable housing financing and achieve a more balanced housing market, particularly in underserved communities.	**Strategic Objective 2B** Preserve quality affordable rental housing, where it is needed most, by simplifying and aligning the delivery of rental housing programs.	**Strategic Objective 3B** Promote advancements in economic prosperity for residents of HUD-assisted housing.	**Strategic Objective 4B** Increase the health and safety of homes and embed comprehensive energy efficiency and healthy housing criteria across HUD programs.
Strategic Objective 1C Restore the Federal Housing Administration's financial health, while supporting the housing market recovery and access to mortgage financing.		**Strategic Objective 3C** Promote the health and housing stability of vulnerable populations.	**Strategic Objective 4C** Support the recovery of communities from disasters by promoting community resilience, developing state and local capacity, and ensuring a coordinated federal response that reduces risk and produces a more resilient built environment.
			Strategic Objective 4D Strengthen communities' economic health, resilience and access to opportunity.

Management Objectives

1. Improve HUD's acquisitions performance through early collaborative planning and enhanced utilization of acquisition tools.
2. Reduce the time and complexity of the clearance process by establishing and enforcing clear protocols for drafting and reviewing documents placed in departmental clearance.
3. Promote a diverse and inclusive work environment that is free of discrimination and harassment by educating the workforce on the overall Equal Employment Opportunity (EEO) process and their EEO responsibilities as managers and employees of HUD.
4. Increase accuracy, speed, transparency, and accountability in financial management and budgeting for the agency.
5. Make the grants management process more efficient and effective by automating and streamlining processes, improving timeliness, and tracking performance.
6. Employ, develop, and foster a collaborative, high-performing workforce that is capable of continuing to deliver HUD's mission in a changing and uncertain future.
7. Make high-quality data available to those who need it, when they need it, where they need it, to support decision-making in furtherance of HUD's mission.
8. Reduce the cost of leased space, utilities, travel, and other related costs by adapting our business processes.

Performance Metrics

Strategic Goal 1: Strengthen the Nation's Housing Market to Bolster the Economy and Protect Consumers

- ► **Strategic Objective 1A: Housing Market**
  - Overall market share of private capital, GSEs, and FHA
- ► **Strategic Objective 1B: Credit Access**
  - Federal Housing Administration share of originations
  - Percent of loans endorsed with credit score < 680
  - Percent of loans endorsed with credit score <680 that evidence successful homeownership over the first five years
  - HUD's Housing Counseling Program clients served
  - Percent of housing counseling clients that gain access to resources to improve their housing situation
- ► **Strategic Objective 1C: FHA's Financial Health**
  - Asset disposition recovery rate
  - Percent of modifications resulting in re-defaults within six months of closing
  - Loss mitigation uptake
  - FHA insured mortgages benefitting from housing counseling

Strategic Goal 2: Meet the Need for Quality Affordable Rental Homes

- ► **Strategic Objective 2A: Rental Investment**
  - Number of households experiencing "Worst Case Housing Needs"
  - Proportion of very low-income renters facing severe rent burdens
  - Percent of rental units built in the preceding four years that had rents below $800
- ► **Strategic Objective 2B: Rental Alignment**
  - Number of families served through HUD rental assistance ✪
  - Number of units converted using the Rental Assistance Demonstration (RAD) ✪
  - Housing Choice Voucher budget utilization rate ✪
  - Public Housing occupancy rate ✪
  - Project Based Rental Assistance (PBRA) occupancy rate ✪
  - Number of units managed under the uniform risk management model
  - Number of inspections saved through inspection sharing

✪ Denotes a measure associated with an Agency Priority Goal (APG)

Performance Metrics (continued)

Strategic Goal 3: Use Housing as a Platform for Improving Quality of Life

▶ **Strategic Objective 3A: Homelessness**
- Total homeless Veterans temporarily living in shelters or transitional housing ✪
- Total Veterans living on the streets, experiencing homelessness ✪
- Veterans placed in permanent housing ✪
- Homeless Veterans served by Continuum of Care resources (transitional housing + Permanent Supportive Housing) ✪
- Individuals experiencing chronic homelessness
- Number and percentage of Permanent Supportive Housing units targeted to individuals experiencing chronic homelessness
- Families experiencing homelessness
- Admissions of new homeless families into HUD-assisted Housing
- Percent of Emergency Solutions Grant dollars dedicated to Rapid Rehousing for homeless families

▶ **Strategic Objective 3B: Economic Prosperity**
- Percent of Section 3 residents hired, of total hiring that occurs as a result of Section 3 covered HUD funding
- Percent of total dollar amount of (construction and non-construction) contracts awarded to Section 3 businesses by covered HUD funding
- Percent of Section 3 covered funding recipients who timely meet reporting, hiring, and contracting requirements
- Number of self-certified Section 3 businesses in HUD's registry nationwide

▶ **Strategic Objective 3C: Health and Housing Stability**
- Number of successful transitions from institutions through Section 811 Project Rental Assistance program
- Percent of HUD-assisted residents with public or private health coverage
- Number of public housing agencies with smoke-free housing policies

Strategic Goal 4: Build Strong, Resilient, and Inclusive Communities

▶ **Strategic Objective 4A: Fair Housing**
- Number of people receiving remedies through Fair Housing Act enforcement work and number of people per case
- Monetary relief per case received through Fair Housing Act enforcement work (for cases with relief less than $100,000)

▶ **Strategic Objective 4B: Green and Healthy Homes**
- Number of HUD-assisted or -associated units completing energy efficient and healthy retrofits or new construction ✪

▶ **Strategic Objective 4C: Disaster Resilience**
- Percent of Sandy Task Force recommendations related to disaster recovery and resilience that have been implemented

▶ **Strategic Objective 4D: Community Development**
- *Metrics under development*

✪ *Denotes a measure associated with an Agency Priority Goal (APG)*

Performance Metrics (continued)

Achieving Operational Excellence: Management Metrics

▶ **Acquisitions**
- Percent requisitions released by the target requisition release date (by Program Office)
- Percent of awards meeting target award date (by the Office of the Chief Procurement Officer)
- Total number of days to contract award, by acquisition strategy

▶ **Departmental Clearance**
- Percent of documents that complete the clearance process by the deadline

▶ **Equal Employment Opportunity**
- Number of pre-complaint resolutions occurring through the Alternate Dispute Resolution process
- Number of complaint filings per fiscal year

▶ **Financial Management**
- *No metrics, but has milestones*

▶ **Grants Management**
- *No metrics, but has milestones*

▶ **Human Capital**
- HUD's score on the Employee Viewpoint Survey Engagement Index
- Percent of succession program positions filled from a pool of well qualified candidates
- Human capital customer satisfaction scores

▶ **Information Technology**
- Number of IT systems
- Cost of IT systems (in millions)
- IT customer service satisfaction scores

▶ **Organizational Structure**
- Amount of money spent on space and travel (in millions)
- Space Utilization (in sq. ft.)

Strategic Goal 1: Strengthen the Nation's Housing Market to Bolster the Economy and Protect Consumers

The state of the housing market plays a large role in stabilizing our neighborhoods and strengthening our national economy. That is why the downturn of the housing market—with high rates of foreclosure, increases in vacant properties, and plummeting home values—was so devastating for families and communities alike. Although the largest factors contributing to this crisis were market-driven—including a slowdown in the growth of home prices, increased high-risk subprime and predatory lending, and lax underwriting standards—the American people turned to Congress and the Administration for leadership and action in righting our nation's housing market. Since the crisis, HUD has played a critical role in this federal recovery strategy—helping American families keep their homes and stabilizing neighborhoods hard hit by foreclosure. HUD seeks to continue to build upon this federal leadership and take a comprehensive approach to tackle the housing crisis by supporting mortgage finance reform legislation. As the housing market continues to recover, HUD will focus on ensuring underserved communities have access to credit while managing risk to the FHA portfolio and doing so in a way that encourages more private investment in the housing market. This work will put HUD in a strong position to minimize the negative impact of any future market disruptions.

- ▶ **Strategic Objective 1A:** Establish a sustainable housing finance system that provides support during market disruptions, with a properly defined role for the US government.

- ▶ **Strategic Objective 1B:** Ensure equal access to sustainable housing financing and achieve a more balanced housing market, particularly in underserved communities.

- ▶ **Strategic Objective 1C:** Restore the Federal Housing Administration's financial health, while supporting the housing market recovery and access to mortgage financing.

Strategic Objective 1A: Housing Market

Establish a sustainable housing finance system that provides support during market disruptions, with a properly defined role for the US government.

OVERVIEW

HUD will work with other agencies, Congress, and stakeholder groups to create a sustainable housing system. In doing so, HUD aims to minimize taxpayer risk by fostering private capital as a primary source of liquidity, and focus governmental participation to a more targeted market of underserved borrowers while still allowing it to maintain its countercyclical role. The right solution will ensure continued access to homeownership and multifamily investment opportunities for creditworthy borrowers while avoiding the problem of private gains and public losses.

STRATEGIES

- **Create a legislative framework to wind down the government-sponsored enterprises (GSE)** in a measured and careful manner. Through this strategy, HUD intends to foster the increased participation of private capital and to insulate taxpayers from losses. At the same time, access to credit must be maintained. In order to accomplish this, HUD will work with Administration partners to lend its expertise in shaping legislative reform.

- **Develop the necessary reforms to focus the Federal Housing Administration on maintaining access to capital** for homeowners and multifamily project owners through all economic cycles. HUD will work to update regulations to allow for access to financing for creditworthy borrowers even during economic downturns.

- **Shape the regulatory landscape through rulemakings.** New rules enhance access to financing for creditworthy borrowers and promote the revival of the private label mortgage sector. This new landscape will also include enhanced safety mechanisms for both consumers and investors.

LEADING THIS OBJECTIVE

Edward Golding

Senior Advisor on Housing Finance

Office of the Secretary

MAJOR MILESTONES

9/30/2015	Support GSE reform bill by 1) developing a legislative framework for GSE reform, 2) providing expertise and technical assistance for legislative efforts to reform housing finance, and 3) supporting a GSE bill which generally meets our objectives as it goes through committee and votes in both bodies of Congress

To track our progress towards this objective, HUD will track the following performance indicator.

► **Overall market share of private capital, Government Sponsored Entities (GSEs), and the Federal Housing Administration (FHA)**
This measure will track the share of the mortgage market for private lenders, government-sponsored entities (Fannie Mae and Freddie Mac), and FHA in order to observe FHA's role in the housing market and the balance of the housing market.

	FY11 Actual	FY12 Actual	FY13 Actual	FY14 Target	FY15 Target
Overall market share of private capital	55.8%	56.2%	No Data	Tracking Only	Tracking Only
Overall market share of GSEs	25.1%	26.3%	No Data	Tracking Only	Tracking Only
Overall market share of FHA/VA	19.2%	17.5%	18.8%	Tracking Only	Tracking Only

Strategic Objective 1B: Credit Access

Ensure access to sustainable housing financing and achieve a more balanced housing market, particularly in underserved communities.

As we recover from the recent downturn in the housing market, equal access to housing financing for creditworthy borrowers in underserved communities continues to be difficult to obtain. For existing homeowners, seriously delinquent loans and underwater loans make it difficult to sell or refinance their home.

For homebuyers, tighter underwriting standards related to additional lender requirements for FHA loans and increased down payment requirements make it harder to obtain a loan. These challenges have disproportionately affected first-time, minority and low-to-moderate income homebuyers and homeowners. HUD will work to ensure that these underserved groups have the ability to get financing.

STRATEGIES

- **Clarify underwriting standards in order to minimize uncertainty in market place.** Increased clarity will encourage access to credit and inhibit risky lender activity. HUD will improve current policies and communicate transparent enforcement and performance standards to industry and stakeholders.

- **Evaluate and align program policies with risk tolerance and mission** to ensure we can help fulfill HUD's mission of providing quality affordable housing. This will be achieved by balancing access/affordability, market factors and the Mutual Mortgage Insurance (MMI) fund in setting price and credit policy.

- **Ensure HUD's Housing Counseling Program reaches as many households as possible, particularly in underserved areas,** so that more households receive information regarding fair housing and fair lending. HUD will do this by making Housing Counseling grants available to housing counseling agencies as soon after appropriation as possible and tracking how many housing counseling clients gain access to resources to help them improve their housing situation due to counseling services.

- **Finalize prospective quality assurance framework and retrospective lender quality assurance enforcement actions** to reduce market uncertainty and improve access to credit.

LEADING THIS OBJECTIVE

Kathleen Zadareky
Acting Deputy Assistant Secretary for Single Family Housing
Office of Housing

Sarah Gerecke
Deputy Assistant Secretary
Office of Housing Counseling

MAJOR MILESTONES

9/30/2014　　**Complete the majority of FHA enforcement actions for loans endorsed prior to December 2011**

9/30/2014　　**Clarify underwriting standards by transitioning from multiple handbooks to a single policy guide**

Underwriting standards are being compiled from multiple sources to one authoritative Single Family Handbook to enhance lender understanding of FHA requirements.

9/30/2015　　**Publish a revised form HUD-9902 for Housing Counseling performance reporting**

The revised form will collect information on access to various forms of housing resources and assistance, including down payment assistance, financing through State Housing Finance Agencies, and rental assistance.

9/30/2015　　**Complete and fully implement new quality assurance framework**

Implement a new QA framework that reduces market uncertainty and improves access to credit

To track our progress towards this objective, HUD will monitor completion of the following performance indicators.

▶ **Federal Housing Administration share of originations**
This measure will show the percentage of mortgage originations in the housing market that were made by Federal Housing Administration.

FY11 Actual	FY12 Actual	FY13 Actual	FY14 Target	FY15 Target
14.8%	13.7%	14.2%	10-15%	10-15%

▶ **Percentage of loans endorsed with credit score < 680**
This measure will track the percentage of FHA loans endorsed that have borrowers with a credit score under 680. Credit scores help lenders to make billions of credit decisions every year. Scores range from 300 to 850.

FY11 Actual	FY12 Actual	FY13 Actual	FY14 Target	FY15 Target
40.0%	42.6%	45.5%	60%	70%

▶ **Percentage of loans endorsed with credit score <680 that evidence successful homeownership over the first five years**

FY11 Actual	FY12 Actual	FY13 Actual	FY14 Target	FY15 Target
No Data	No Data	No Data	NA	Establish Baseline

▶ **HUD's Housing Counseling Program clients served**
This measure will track the incremental number each year of clients counseled through the HUD Housing Counseling program. Learn more about the Office of Housing Counseling and the assistance it offers.

FY11 Actual	FY12 Actual	FY13 Actual	FY14 Target	FY15 Target
1,900,575	1,657,147	1,567,530	1,500,000	2,000,000

▶ **Percentage of housing counseling clients that gain access to resources to improve their housing situation**
This measure will track the percentage of housing counseling clients who gain access to resources to help them improve their housing situation (e.g. down payment assistance, rental assistance) as a direct result of receiving Housing Counseling Services.

FY11 Actual	FY12 Actual	FY13 Actual	FY14 Target	FY15 Target
No Data	No Data	No Data	NA	Establish Baseline

Strategic Objective 1C: FHA's Financial Health

> **Restore the Federal Housing Administration's financial health, while supporting the housing market recovery and access to mortgage financing.**

OVERVIEW

A strong Federal Housing Administration (FHA) is critical to the recovery of the housing market and our economy at large. The mortgage insurance provided by FHA has made financing available to individuals and families not adequately served by the conventional private mortgage market. The Mutual Mortgage Insurance Fund is the largest fund covering activities of FHA. The recession put substantial strain on the MMIF as private capital retreated and FHA played a countercyclical role to support the broader housing market. Over time, FHA has experienced significant swings in its market share as it has stepped in to provide capital for qualified borrowers who would otherwise be shut out of the mortgage market.

In addition, the severe decline in house prices, the sluggish performance of the economy, and the behavior of some lending partners resulted in increased FHA losses that drove its excess capital reserve ratio[1] below the congressionally mandated 2 percent level.

STRATEGIES

- **Restore FHA's excess capital reserve ratio** to the congressionally mandated 2 percent level by 2015. Strengthen FHA's book of business through policy reforms and minimize losses on existing books.

- **Continue loss mitigation efforts in order to prevent foreclosures**. Focus on effective and proactive loss mitigation. HUD will track the effectiveness of these efforts by measuring the number of homeowners who re-default after receiving assistance.

- **Maximize Real Estate Owned (REO) recovery rate** by enhancing contractor performance through use of a scorecard and implementing a best execution model across all asset disposition options.

- **Increase the number of FHA-insured mortgages for which the borrower received either pre-purchase or post-purchase housing counseling** in order to improve outcomes for FHA-insured borrowers and strengthen the health of the Mutual Mortgage Insurance (MMI) fund.

---

[1] The capital ratio compares the "economic net worth" of the MMI Fund to the dollar balance of active, insured loans, at a point in time. Economic net worth is defined as a net asset position, where the present value of expected future revenues and net claim expenses is added to current balance sheet positions. The capital ratio computation is part of an annual valuation of the outstanding portfolio of insured loans at the end of each fiscal year.

LEADING THIS OBJECTIVE

Kathleen Zadareky
Acting Deputy Assistant Secretary for Single Family Housing
Office of Housing

Sarah Gerecke
Deputy Assistant Secretary
Office of Housing Counseling

MAJOR MILESTONES

6/30/2014	Implement asset execution model that ensures that the Federal Housing Administration realizes optimal recovery across all disposition options
6/30/2014	Measure and maximize management and marketing contractor performance by rolling out initial performance scorecards
9/30/2014	Develop a loan servicing contractor scorecard for Secretary-held loan servicing
9/30/2014	Design and implement appropriate analytical models to estimate interim actuarial results
9/30/2015	Implement comprehensive policies through Mortgagee Letters and rulemaking that will eliminate negative capital reserve on Mutual Mortgage Insurance Home Equity Conversion Mortgage (HECM) portfolio

MEASURING OUR PROGRESS

To track our progress towards this objective, HUD will monitor progress towards the following performance indicators.

▶ **Asset disposition recovery rate**

This is the net recovery rate that FHA realizes on the sale of assets as a percentage of claim payment.

FY11 Results	FY12 Results	FY13 Results	FY14 Target	FY15 Target
45%	38%	43%	45%	5% increase (relative to FY14)

▶ **Percentage of modifications resulting in re-defaults within 6 months of closing**

This measure will track the percentage of borrowers that become 90 days or more delinquent on their loans within 6 months of receiving a loan modification/FHA Home Affordable Modification Program (HAMP) modification.

FY11 Results	FY12 Results	FY13 Results	FY14 Target	FY15 Target
13.6%	13.5%	0.4%	0.4%	2% reduction (relative to FY14)

▶ **Loss mitigation uptake**

This is the percentage of loss mitigation actions taken as a percent of serious mortgage delinquencies. Loss mitigation programs are typically used to assist homeowners who have been in default on their mortgage payments for over 90 days (serious delinquency). Examples include the FHA Home Affordable Modification Program, special forbearance, mortgage modifications, partial claims, pre-foreclosure sales, and deeds in lieu. This is important because finding a loss mitigation solution—such as a loan modification or a partial claim—is a better outcome than foreclosure, for both the borrower and FHA. Learn more about loss mitigation

FY11 Results	FY12 Results	FY13 Results	FY14 Target	FY15 Target
21.5%	15.9%	19.3%	20%	20%

▶ **Number of FHA insured mortgages benefitting from housing counseling**

This is the number of FHA borrowers that receive pre- or post-purchase counseling.

FY11 Results	FY12 Results	FY13 Results	FY14 Target	FY15 Target
No Data	No Data	No Data	NA	Establish Baseline

▶ **Capital Reserve Ratio**

The capital ratio compares the "economic net worth" of the MMI Fund to the dollar balance of active, insured loans, at a point in time. Economic net worth is defined as a net asset position, where the present value of expected future revenues and net claim expenses is added to current balance sheet positions. The capital ratio computation is part of an annual valuation of the outstanding portfolio of insured loans at the end of each fiscal year.

FY11 Results	FY12 Results	FY13 Results	FY14 Target	FY15 Target
0.24%	-1.44%	-0.11%	1.2%	2.0%

Retrospective: FY 2012-2013 Agency Priority Goal · Foreclosure Prevention
Between October 1, 2011 and September 30, 2013, HUD aimed to assist 700,000 homeowners who were
at risk of losing their homes due to foreclosure. HUD exceeded this goal by 238,734 homeowners (34%).

	Target	Actual	Change from Previous Year	Target Met?

☼ Homeowners assisted through early delinquency interventions†

Early delinquency interventions are typically used to assist homeowners who have been in default on their mortgage payments for less than 90 days. Providing assistance to homeowners who are in the early stages of mortgage payment distress can avert the potential for more serious delinquencies, defaults, and foreclosures at a later date. Examples of these interventions include repayment (in which the borrower agrees to repay delinquent amounts to bring the mortgage current) and trial modification.

	Target	Actual	Change from Previous Year	Target Met?
2009	--	191,351	--	NA
2010	200,000	213,403	+22,052 (↑12%)	✓
2011	200,000	202,794	+09,391 (↑33%)	✓
2012	250,000	290,216	+7,422 (↑3%)	✓
2013	250,000	309,339	+19,123 (↑7%)	✓
net change, 2009 – 2013			+1,287,103 homeowners assisted	

☼ Homeowners assisted through loss mitigation†

Loss mitigation programs are typically used to assist homeowners who have been in default on their mortgage payments for over 90 days. Examples include the FHA Home Affordable Modification Program, special forbearance, mortgage modifications, partial claims, preforeclosure sales, and deeds in lieu. This is important because finding a loss mitigation solution—such as a loan modification or a partial claim—is a better outcome than foreclosure, for both the borrower and FHA. | Learn more about loss mitigation

	Target	Actual	Change from Previous Year	Target Met?
2009	--	130,358	--	NA
2010	162,015	193,344	+62,986 (↑48%)	✓
2011	137,985	212,890	+19,546 (↑10%)	✓
2012	100,000	154,933	-57,957 (↓27%)	✓
2013	100,000	184,246	+29,313 (↑19%)	✓
net change, 2009 – 2013			+875,771 homeowners assisted	

☼ Total homeowners assisted† (early delinquency interventions + loss mitigation actions)

	Target	Actual	Change from Previous Year	Target Met?
2009	--	321,709	--	NA
2010	362,015	406,747	+85,038 (↑26%)	✓
2011	337,985	495,684	+88,937 (↑21%)	✓
2012	350,000	445,149	-50,535 (↓10%)	✓
2013	350,000	493,585	+48,436 (↑11%)	✓
2012+2013 combined	700,000	938,734		✓
net change, 2009 – 2013			+2,162,874 homeowners assisted	

†Annual performance represents progress achieved during each fiscal year, October 1st to September 30th

	Target	Actual	Change from Previous Year	Target Met?

✧ Consolidated claims workout ratio†

The consolidated claims workout ratio, or "CCW ratio," measures what proportion of FHA loss mitigation and foreclosure claims paid consisted specifically of loss mitigation claims. This means that the <u>higher</u> the ratio, the greater the proportion of loss mitigation claims were paid out *instead* of foreclosure claims. This is important because finding a loss mitigation solution—such as a loan modification or a partial claim—is a better outcome than foreclosure, for both the borrower and FHA. (should ideally stay stable or increase over time)

	Target	Actual	Change from Previous Year	Target Met?
2009	--	66	--	NA
2010	68	67	+1% point	✗
2011	75	72	+5% points	✗
2012	50	63	-9% points	✓
2013	50	65	+2% points	✓
net change, 2009 – 2013			decrease of 1 percentage point	

✧ 6-month re-default rate†

For those homeowners who were at risk of foreclosure and received loss mitigation support, we track the rate of re-default on their mortgage payments within the first 6 months after receiving the loss mitigation assistance. This measure provides important insights because most re-defaults on mortgage payments tend to occur within the first 6 months after receiving an intervention. (should ideally decrease over time)

	Target	Actual	Change from Previous Year	Target Met?
2009	--	26%	--	NA
2010	23%	18%	-8% points	✓
2011	20%	14%	-4% points	✓
2012	13%	13%	-1% points	✓
2013	10%	8%	-5% points	✓
net change, 2009 – 2013			decrease of 18 percentage points	

† Annual performance represents progress achieved during each fiscal year, October 1st to September 30th

Retrospective: FY 2012-2013 Agency Priority Goal · Foreclosure Prevention

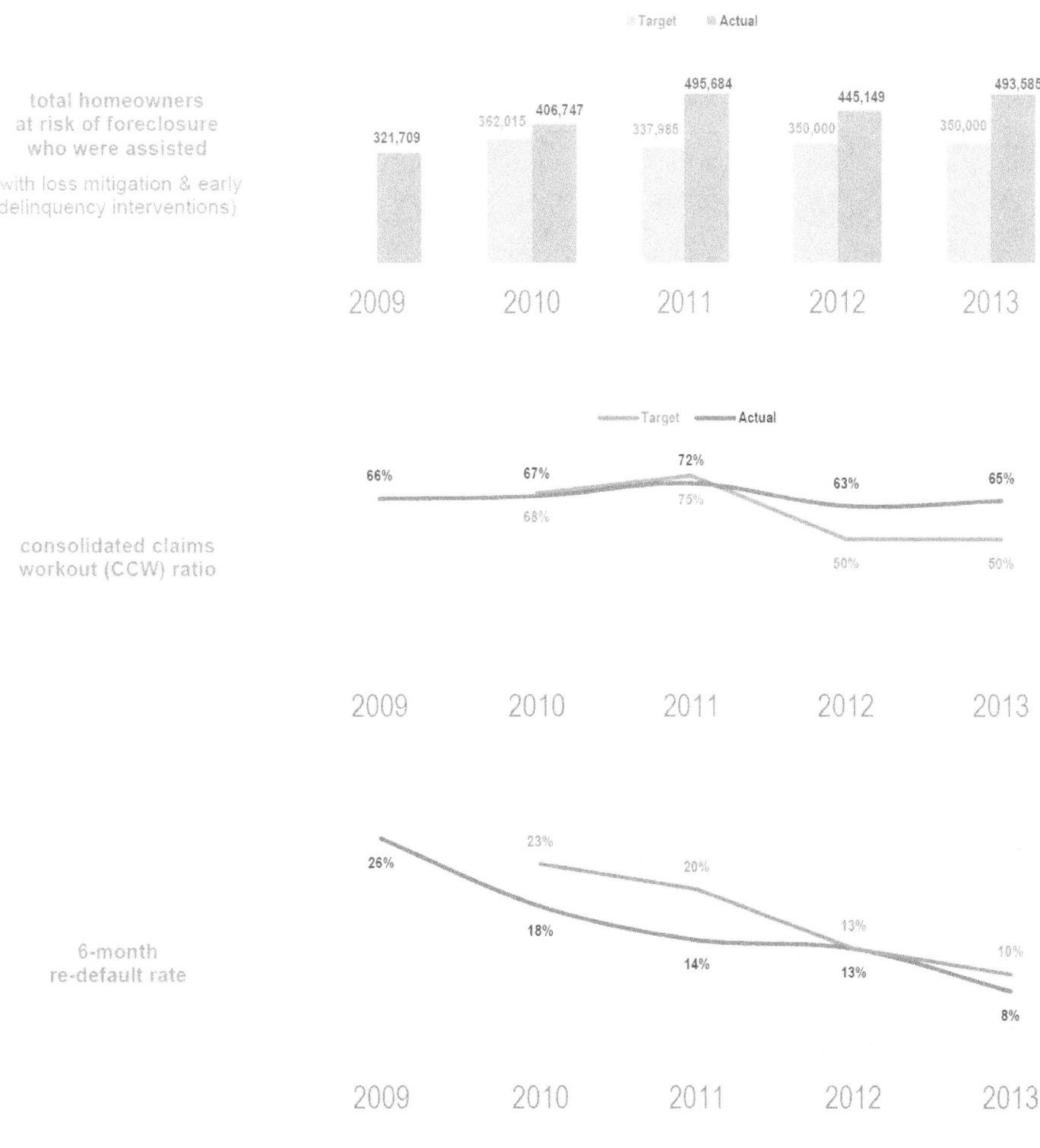

total homeowners
at risk of foreclosure
who were assisted

(with loss mitigation & early
delinquency interventions)

Target   Actual

	2009	2010	2011	2012	2013
Target		362,015	337,985	350,000	350,000
Actual	321,709	406,747	495,684	445,149	493,585

consolidated claims
workout (CCW) ratio

Target   Actual

Actual: 66% (2009), 67% (2010), 72% (2011), 63% (2012), 65% (2013)
Target: 68% (2010), 75% (2011), 50% (2012), 50% (2013)

6-month
re-default rate

26% (2009), 18% (2010), 14% (2011), 13% (2012), 8% (2013)
23% (2010), 20% (2011), 13% (2012), 10% (2013)

Between October 1, 2011 and September 30, 2013, HUD set a priority goal of assisting 700,000 homeowners who were at risk of losing their homes due to foreclosure. In that two-year period, HUD exceeded its target by 34%, assisting 238,734 more homeowners than planned. HUD exceeded cumulative targets for early delinquency interventions and loss mitigation actions by 20 percent and 70 percent, respectively, for a total of 938,734 homeowners assisted. HUD also performed well on its supporting measures: At the end of FY 2013, the consolidated claims workout (CCW) ratio of 65% exceeded our target, and the six-month re-default rate was at its lowest point in the past five years—a decrease of 18 percentage points since 2009. The six-month re-default rate is the percent of homeowners who have re-defaulted on their mortgages within six months of receiving loss mitigation assistance.

Our success on this goal is due to our continued work with lenders to find ways to help borrowers at risk for foreclosure as well as outreach to borrowers to ensure they are aware of their options when facing foreclosure. Although our performance is strong, the high number of homeowners who are in default for more than 90 days that may go into foreclosure continues to be an issue that we are monitoring closely and that may affect our Consolidated Claims Workout Ratio moving forward.

Although unemployment has decreased over time, sustained unemployment is the most significant barrier to mitigating the crisis and is subject to macroeconomic conditions that cannot be controlled by the Department. The programs contributing to this goal aim to keep individuals in their homes by lowering their monthly mortgage payments. However, borrowers must still earn enough monthly income to afford the modified payments. Individuals who have lost their jobs or who have faced significant reductions in their income may still not be able to afford even modified monthly payments.

All of these programs rely on cooperation with and implementation through third party mortgage servicers and lenders. As such, the rate and volume of assistance provided to eligible homeowners is subject to the infrastructure and customer service administered by these third parties. The Department and the Administration as a whole have taken several steps to partner with and assist the industry to help as many homeowners as possible.

For detailed quarterly assessments of progress from 2012-2013, readers may consult the archived quarterly updates on **Performance.gov**. These measures are not being continued as specific agency priority goals in the FY 2014-2015 performance period, but other measures will be used to monitor HUD's progress towards restoring the Federal Housing Administration's financial health, supporting the recovery, and supporting access to financing.

Retrospective: FY 2012-2013 Agency Priority Goal · Vacancy Rate Reduction

Between October 1, 2011 and September 30, 2013, HUD aimed to reduce the average residential vacancy rate in 70 percent of the neighborhoods hardest hit by the foreclosure crisis relative to comparable areas. This goal was exceeded by four percentage points.

	Target	Actual	Change from Previous Year	Target Met?

✪ Percent of Neighborhood Investment Clusters (NICs) with improved vacancy rate outcomes over at least one comparable area†

This indicator identifies NICs (neighborhoods with at least 2 NSP investments per 100 houses) and tracks their vacancy rates against comparable (in terms of vacancy rate, home price, and market conditions pre-2008) neighborhoods that received no investment.

	Target	Actual	Change from Previous Year	Target Met?
2012	70%	75%	NA	✓
2013	70%	74%	(↓1%)	✓

✪ NSP2 target areas units of service†

This is the number of units of service completed and occupied using Neighborhood Stabilization Program Round 2 (NSP2) funds, as reported by NSP2 grantees. Units of service are the number of units produced within each eligible activity. Many units may be produced with multiple activities (e.g., acquisition and rehab) and therefore the measure "units of service" is not directly translatable into number of total individual housing units.

	Target	Actual	Change from Previous Year	Target Met?
2012	6,157	5,292	NA	✗
2013	13,305	5,884	+592 (↑11%)	✗
net change, 2012 – 2013			+11,176 units of service	

✪ Average days to list REO properties to market†

HUD acquires residential properties (1 to 4 units per property) when owners default and lenders foreclose on mortgages insured by the Federal Housing Administration (FHA). These acquired properties become Departmental assets, and are referred to as Real Estate Owned (REO) properties. To help rebuild neighborhoods that have been struggling with blight and declining home values due to foreclosures, local communities—through the National First Look program—receive a brief, exclusive opportunity to purchase bank-owned properties in certain neighborhoods so these homes can be rehabilitated, rented, resold, or demolished. This particular measure is the average number of days it takes to list a Federal Housing Administration (FHA) Real Estate Owned (REO) property to the market. Good performance would see this number decreasing.

	Target	Actual	Change from Previous Year	Target Met?
2012	44	22	NA	✓
2013	22	21	↓1 day	✓
net change, 2012 – 2013	reduced average days to list by 8 days, *relative to first quarter of FY 2012*			

✪ Average time in inventory for REO properties†

This it the average number of days a Federal Housing Administration (FHA) Real Estate Owned (REO) property stays in the inventory. Good performance would see this number decreasing.

	Target	Actual	Change from Previous Year	Target Met?
2012	188	136	NA	✓
2013	136	120	↓16 days	✓
net change, 2012 – 2013	reduced average days in inventory by 52 days, *relative to first quarter of FY 2012*			

†Annual performance represents progress achieved during each fiscal year, October 1st to September 30th

Retrospective: FY 2012-2013 Agency Priority Goal · Vacancy Rate Reduction

Target   Actual

percent of Neighborhood Investment Clusters (NICs) with improved vacancy rate outcomes over at least one comparable area

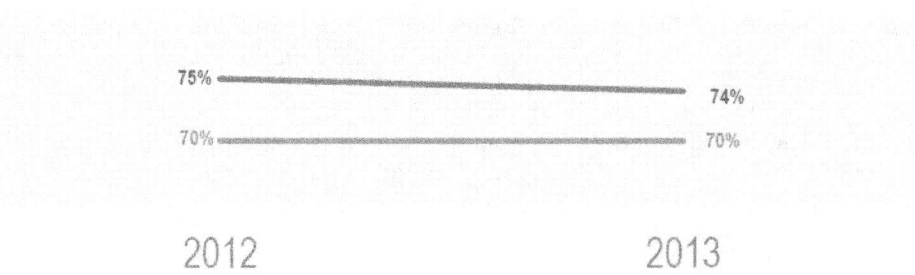

Neighborhood Stabilization Program (NSP) 2 target areas: units of service

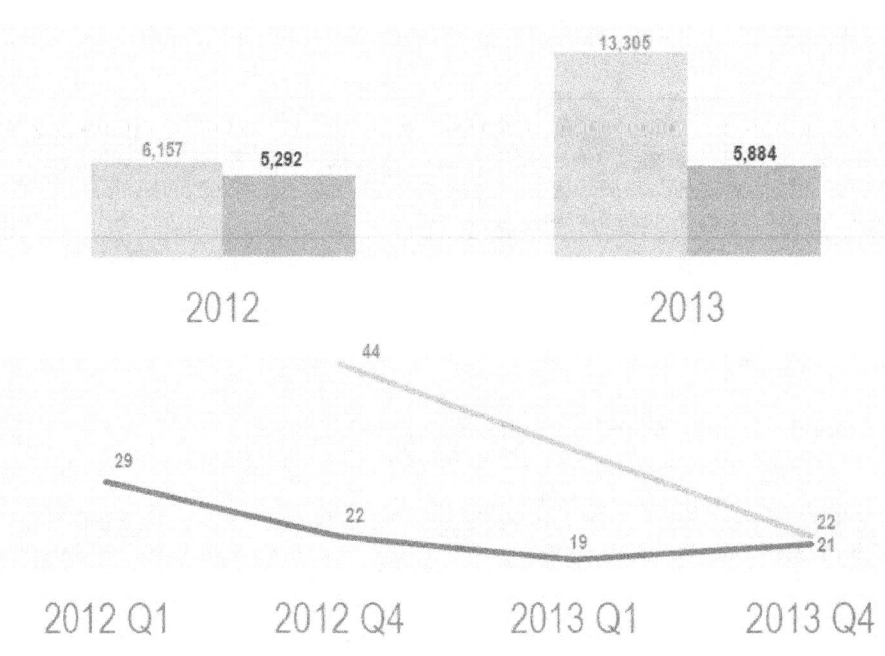

average days to list Real Estate Owned (REO) properties to market

average time in inventory for Real Estate Owned (REO) properties

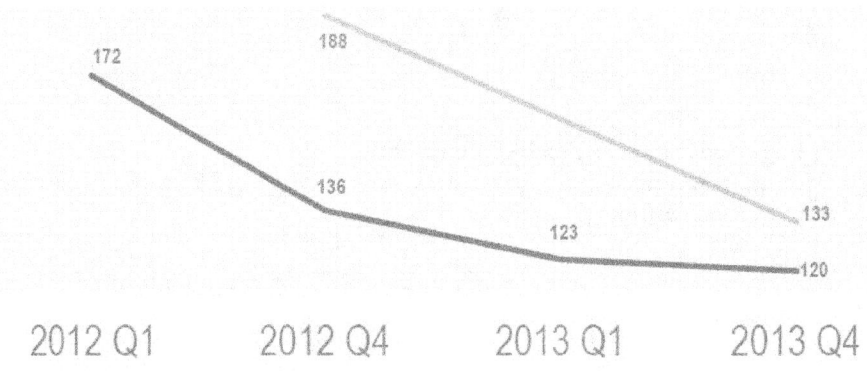

FINAL PROGRESS UPDATE

Between October 1, 2011 and September 30, 2013, HUD aimed to reduce the average residential vacancy rate in 70 percent of the neighborhoods hardest hit by the foreclosure crisis relative to comparable areas. By the end of 2013, HUD exceeded its target on its key measure, as well as its targets on two of three supporting metrics.

- By the end of FY 2013, HUD exceeded its target for the percentage of Neighborhood Investment Clusters (NICs) beating at least one comparable by four percentage points. This means that 74 percent of neighborhoods with at least two Neighborhood Stabilization Program ("NSP2") investments per 100 houses demonstrated lower average residential vacancy rates compared to similar neighborhoods (in terms of factors like home prices and market conditions pre-2008) that received no Neighborhood Stabilization Program investment. The second round of funding for the Neighborhood Stabilization Program, or "NSP2," is HUD's primary tool for stabilizing neighborhoods whose viability has been and continues to be damaged by the economic effects of properties that have been foreclosed upon and abandoned. "NSP2" specifically references the grant funds provided by the American Recovery and Reinvestment Act of 2009 (P.L. No. 111-5) to states, local governments, nonprofits, and a consortium of public and/or private nonprofit entities on a competitive basis. For more information about this measure, please visit Performance.gov.

- By the end of FY 2013, the number of units serviced through the Neighborhood Stabilization Program 2 was lower than originally anticipated, but the units of service continue to be counted through this funding, beyond September 2013. Of 19,462 units expected to be completed by end of FY 2013, 11,176 (54%) were finished by that time. By statute, NSP2 grantees were required to expend all grant funds by February 11, 2013, but units are not counted until they are occupied. Therefore, the production estimates will lag expenditures by 6-18 months, and we can expect more completions to occur through approximately August 2014.

- Between FY2012–FY 2013, significant reductions were made in the average number of days a Federal Housing Administration (FHA) Real Estate Owned (REO) property stayed in the inventory (reduction by 52 days), as well as the average time to list such properties to the market (reduction by 8 days). HUD staff that manage FHA REO properties continue to find ways to make the listing and selling process more efficient.

The continued provision of technical assistance (TA) relies on the use of Neighborhood Stabilization Program (Round 3) TA funds, which are not authorized to serve NSP2 grantees—an issue that CPD is currently working to address. Market conditions are also a large factor for NSP2 grantees, which face still-declining property values, competition from investors, reluctance from lenders, and local capacity issues related to tight budgets, and TA may be needed to help these grantees successfully implement their programs.

For detailed quarterly assessments of progress from 2012-2013, readers may consult the archived quarterly updates on Performance.gov. These measures are not being continued as specific agency priority goals in the FY 2014-2015 performance period, but other measures will be used to monitor HUD's progress towards Strategic Goal 1.

Strategic Goal 2: Meet the Need for Quality Affordable Rental Homes

Renters in America face serious difficulty finding affordable housing in a broad range of communities because of the dual problems of a shortage of units in some areas and a lack of income to afford units in the existing market. Despite the units of housing provided through HUD's programs, the supply of affordable and available rental housing in America is insufficient. Moreover, the number of families struggling to make ends meet in the face of severe rent burdens continues to increase. HUD remains committed to providing rental assistance to poor households within this challenging environment.

- ▶ **Strategic Objective 2A:** Ensure sustainable investments in affordable rental housing.

- ▶ **Strategic Objective 2B:** Preserve quality affordable rental housing, where it is needed most, by simplifying and aligning the delivery of rental housing programs.

Strategic Objective 2A: Rental Investment

Ensure sustainable investments in affordable rental housing.

OVERVIEW

According to the latest American Community Survey, the number of households earning under $15,000 a year and paying more than half their incomes for housing increased by 1.5 million in 2007–10, nearly doubling the increase from 2001–2007. The scale of this problem, and others presented in the *Worst Case Housing Needs 2011*[2] study, requires major strategic decisions. As worst case housing needs continue to increase and the level of housing assistance remains relatively flat, the gap between the number of assisted units and the number of households with severe housing needs has never been wider. It is critical to grow the level of private investment into affordable housing. Currently, for every very low-income household that receives rental assistance, there are nearly two very low-income households with worst case housing needs. Individuals and families are considered to have "worst case housing needs" when they have incomes below 50 percent of the Area Median Income (AMI), do not receive government assistance, and either pay more than one-half their income on rent, live in severely inadequate conditions, or face both of these challenges.

STRATEGIES

- **Pursue Housing Finance Reform legislation**. HUD will continue working with Administration partners and Congress to support housing finance reform legislation that provides liquidity and capital to support affordable rental financing and that creates a dedicated, budget-neutral financing mechanism to support affordable rental housing and access to homeownership for low-income families.

- **Implement the Housing Trust Fund and support the Capital Magnet Fund**. HERA required the establishment and management of a Capital Magnet Fund and a Housing Trust Fund, the latter to be directed by the Secretary of the US Department of Housing and Urban Development. The Housing Trust fund is to be supported by amounts that may be appropriated, transferred, or credited to such fund under any other provision of law. HERA specified that the housing trust funds would come from the Federal National Mortgage Association and the Federal Home Loan Mortgage Corporation. That plan, however, was delayed as a result of the financial challenges of those agencies. As these entities restore their fiscal health and as the Administration works with Congress on enacting comprehensive housing finance reform, or capitalizing the Housing Trust Fund with direct appropriations, this strategic objective will assist in moving both initiatives forward.

LEADING THIS OBJECTIVE

Ben Metcalf
Deputy Assistant Secretary
Office of Multifamily Housing

---

[2] U.S. Department of Housing and Urban Development, 2013 (August); *Worst Case Housing Needs 2011: Report to Congress.*

MAJOR MILESTONES

9/30/2014	Publication of the Housing Trust Fund Final Rule

MEASURING OUR PROGRESS

HUD will track performance on the following indicators:

- ► **Number of households experiencing "Worst Case Housing Needs"** (key measure)
  The term "worst case housing needs" is defined as very low-income renters (with incomes below 50 percent of the Area Median Income) who do not receive government housing assistance and who either paid more than half of their income for rent or lived in severely inadequate conditions, or who faced both of these challenges. HUD's estimates of worst case needs are based primarily on data from the American Housing Survey (AHS).

FY11 Actual	FY12 Actual	FY13 Actual	FY14 Target	FY15 Target
8.48 million[3]	No Data[4]	No Data[5]	Tracking Only	Tracking Only

- ► **Proportion of very low-income renters facing severe rent burdens** (contextual indicator)
  This measure is based on American Community Survey data and tracks the proportion of very low-income renters (with incomes below 50 percent of the Area Median Income), who spend more than 50% or more of their income on rent.

FY11 Actual	FY12 Actual	FY13 Actual	FY14 Target	FY15 Target
49.2%[6]	No Data	No Data	Tracking Only	Tracking Only

- ► **Percentage of rental units built in the preceding four years that had rents below $800,** which are affordable for the median renter, prepared using American Housing Survey data. (contextual indicator)

FY11 Actual	FY12 Actual	FY13 Actual	FY14 Target	FY15 Target
34%	No Data	No Data	Tracking Only	Tracking Only

---

[3] *Worst Case Housing Needs 2011 Report to Congress* (http://www.huduser.org/Publications/pdf/HUD-506_WorstCase2011_reportv3.pdf) (Exhibit 1.9). This figure was 7.095 million in 2009.

[4] Data on worst case housing needs are published every other year.

[5] Data on FY 2013 will be published in 2015.

[6] *Worst Case Housing Needs 2011 Report to Congress* (http://www.huduser.org/Publications/pdf/HUD-506_WorstCase2011_reportv3.pdf) (Table A-5A). This figure was 47.6% in 2009.

Strategic Objective 2B: Rental Alignment

Preserve availability of quality affordable rental housing, where it is needed most, by simplifying and aligning the delivery of rental housing programs.

OVERVIEW

During the past 75 years, the federal government has invested billions of dollars in the development and maintenance of affordable public and multifamily housing. Despite the sizable investment and the great demand for affordable rental housing, units continue to be lost. While some units have been lost because of their deteriorated physical condition, others, both publically and privately owned, have been removed from the affordable inventory because of owners' decisions or because periods of affordability have expired. Some multifamily housing programs either have no option for owners to renew their subsidy contracts with HUD or cannot renew on terms that attract sufficient capital to preserve long-term affordability. Moreover, the public housing stock faces an estimated $26 billion capital needs backlog that will be difficult to meet given federal fiscal constraints.

HUD's Rental Assistance Demonstration (RAD) makes it possible for public housing agencies to address the immediate and longer-term capital repair and replacement needs of their properties, preserving these deeply affordable rental homes. RAD allows access to private funding sources by allowing public housing agencies and owners of Moderate Rehabilitation, Rent Supplement, and Rental Assistance Payment developments to convert to long-term Section 8 rental assistance contracts.

The preservation of an even broader range of HUD-assisted properties will be facilitated by the establishment of a Recapitalization Office that will handle a variety of complicated preservation transactions, providing a "one stop shop" for owners in order to minimize program complexity, from their perspective. Moreover, HUD's participation in the White House Rental Policy Working Group has spurred improvements in rental housing across agencies, particularly in the area of unit physical inspections and HUD's Real Estate Assessment Center's role.

STRATEGIES

- **Establish the Recapitalization Office**, to reposition HUD-assisted multifamily and public housing assets to revitalize neighborhoods and preserve affordable housing to improve opportunities for residents. The office will bring staff and programs used by common partners together to support affordable housing and improve neighborhoods, including RAD, Choice Neighborhoods, HOPE VI, mixed-finance public housing, demolition/disposition, Promise Zones, Mark-to-Market, Section 202 and 236 transactions, and other recapitalization activities. This office will better integrate place-based initiatives and provide more useful interactions with our external partners who are using programs throughout HUD to develop and reposition their assets.

- **Develop and adopt a uniform asset management model across program platforms and divisions**, considering existing legislative and regulatory requirements. By using both property-level oversight and counterparty entity oversight, a uniform asset risk assessment management model will help to ensure consistent timely interventions and minimize risk.

- **Revise the Real Estate Assessment Center's** scoring system, timeframes and operation of physical and financial assessments of HUD-assisted properties.

- **Support the development and preservation of affordable housing through FHA Multifamily Mortgage Insurance**, in conjunction with other funding or financial resources such as through the FHA Low Income Housing Tax Credit (LIHTC) pilot.

- **Ensure that the households currently being served by HUD rental assistance programs are able to remain housed in their assisted properties.**
    - Create a proactive asset management approach to work with owners prior to contract expiration/mortgage maturity to develop a preservation strategy for the property.
    - Preserve units, maintain high occupancy and utilization rates, and reduce the number of units converted to market rate housing.

- **Implement and expand the Rental Assistance Demonstration (RAD)** to preserve and transition existing affordable HUD-assisted rental units to the Section 8 platform.

LEADING THIS OBJECTIVE
> Ben Metcalf
> *Deputy Assistant Secretary*
> Office of Multifamily Housing
>
> Ophelia Basgal
> *Region IX Administrator*
> (California/Pacific/Hawaii)
>
> Lindsey Reames
> *Acting Deputy Assistant Secretary*
> Office of Field Operations
> Office of Public and Indian Housing

MAJOR MILESTONES

9/30/2014	**Develop a consolidated rental housing risk model** to be used by the Office of Public Housing and the Office of Multifamily Housing
9/1/2015	**Provide guidance and technical assistance on monitoring and inspecting HOME projects**, to include instructions about how Participating Jurisdictions can align with other funding partners during the Period of Affordability

MEASURING OUR PROGRESS

HUD will monitor performance of the following performance indicators:

○ Fiscal Year 2014-2015 Agency Priority Goal:

Between October 1, 2013 and September 30, 2015, HUD aims to preserve and expand affordable rental housing through its rental housing programs.

▶ ○ **Number of families served through HUD rental assistance** (key indicator)

FY11 Actual	FY12 Actual	FY13 Actual	FY14 Target	FY15 Target
5,340,320	5,447,499	5,467,975	5,516,620	5,589,920

▶ ○ **Number of units converted using the Rental Assistance Demonstration (RAD): First Component**[7] (supporting indicator)

FY11 Actual	FY12 Actual	FY13 Actual	FY14 Target	FY15 Target
NA	NA	32	15,000	21,000

▶ ○ **Number of units converted using the Rental Assistance Demonstration (RAD): Second Component**[8] (supporting indicator)

FY11 Actual	FY12 Actual	FY13 Actual	FY14 Target	FY15 Target
NA	NA	4,4,789	5,161	Target TBD

▶ ○ **Housing Choice Voucher budget utilization rate** (supporting indicator)
This is the calendar year to date Housing Assistance Payment (HAP) spending as a percent of calendar year to date budget authority.

FY11 Actual	FY12 Actual	FY13 Actual	FY14 Target	FY15 Target
99.8%	99.04%	103.48%	97.56%	Target TBD

---

[7] The *first component* of the Rental Assistance Demonstration allows projects funded under the public housing and Section 8 Moderate Rehabilitation (Mod Rehab) programs to convert their assistance to long-term, project-based Section 8 rental assistance contracts. Under this component of RAD, public housing agencies (PHAs) and Mod Rehab owners may choose between two forms of Section 8 Housing Assistance Payment (HAP) contracts: project-based vouchers (PBVs) or project-based rental assistance (PBRA).

[8] The *second component* of the Rental Assistance Demonstration allows owners of projects funded under the Rent Supplement (Rent Supp), Rental Assistance Payment (RAP), and Mod Rehab programs to convert tenant protection vouchers (TPVs) to project-based vouchers (PBVs). The FY14 target includes 3,661 units remaining to be converted at the end of FY13 as well as 1,500 new units under extended authority for 2014.

▶ ◯ Public Housing occupancy rate

FY11 Actual	FY12 Actual	FY13 Actual	FY14 Target	FY15 Target
95%	96%	96%	96%	96%

▶ ◯ Project Based Rental Assistance (PBRA) occupancy rate

FY11 Actual	FY12 Actual	FY13 Actual	FY14 Target	FY15 Target
94.8%	95.1%	95.2%	Tracking Only	Tracking Only

Other Measures:

▶ Number of units managed under the uniform risk management model

FY11 Actual	FY12 Actual	FY13 Actual	FY14 Target	FY15 Target
No Data*	No Data*	No Data*	Establish Baseline	Target TBD

*First results will not be available until September 2014.

▶ Number of inspections saved through inspection sharing

FY11 Actual	FY12 Actual	FY13 Actual	FY14 Target	FY15 Target
No Data	No Data	102*	Establish Baseline	Target TBD

*Actual inspections saved during pilot, with participation by six states.

Retrospective: FY 2012-2013 Agency Priority Goal – Affordable Rental Housing

Between October 1, 2011 and September 30, 2013, HUD aimed to preserve affordable rental housing by continuing to serve 5.4 million total families and serve an additional 61,000 families through HUD's affordable rental housing programs. HUD exceeded this goal by nearly 82,000 families.

	Target	Actual	Change from Previous Year	Target Met?
Additional families housed in affordable rental housing				
This indicator tracks the total number of additional households served since the beginning of the performance period.				
2010	79,191	51,160	--	✗
2011	127,828	98,267	+47,107 (↑92%)	✗
2012	29,869	108,940	+10,673 (↑11%)	✓
2013	31,591	34,026	-74,914 (↓69%)	✓
2012+2013 combined	61,460	142,966		✓
net change, 2010 – 2013			+292,393 additional families housed	

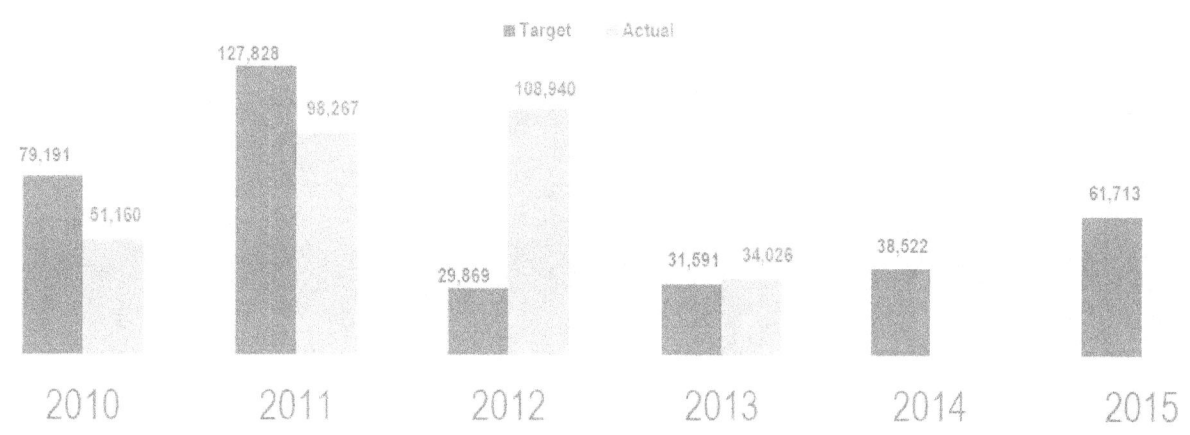

Program	FY 2011 Cumulative Baseline	FY 2012 Incremental Actual	FY 2012 Cumulative Actual	FY 2013 Incremental Actual	FY 2013 Cumulative Baseline	FY 2014 Incremental Target	FY 2014 Cumulative Target	FY 2015 Incremental Target	FY 2015 Cumulative Target
Multifamily Project Based Rental Assistance[10]	1,179,327	(4,413)	1,174,914	(3,822)	1 171,092	(5,945)	1,165,147	(6,963)	1,158,184
Rental Assistance Demonstration units move to PBRA	-	-	-	15	15	7,125	7,140	9,975	17,115
Other Multifamily Subsidies[11]	178,532	(7,316)	171,216	(4,870)	166,346	(12,000)	154,346	(12,000)	142,346
Project Rental Assistance Contract (Sect. 202 & 811)	140,445	2,532	142,977	3,547	146,524	2,568	149,092	2,780	151,872
Insured Tax Exempt or Low-Income Housing Tax Credit	114,546	9,041	123,587	2,578	126,165	35,635[12]	161,800	39,187	200,987
Mortgage Insurance for Residential Care Facilities (Sect. 232)[13]	460	1,920	2,380	1,948	4,328	750	5,078	750	5,828
TOTAL Housing Programs	1,613,310	1,764	1,615,074	(604)	1,614,470	18,788	1,630,972	22,142	1,653,114
PIH Mainstream and Tenant Based Rental Assistance	2,183,276	24,448	2,207,724	(14,179)	2,193,545	2,758	2,196,303	48,230	2,244,533
Rental Assistance Demonstration units move to TBRA	-	-	-	4,565	4,565	12,028	16,593	11,400	27,993
Public Housing[14]	1,082,393	9,365	1,091,758	(1,287)	1,090,471	(18,473)	1,071,998	(39,127)	1,032,871
Indian Housing Block Grant	10,615	854	11,469	416	11,885	594	12,479	594	13,073
PIH Mod Rehab	23,398	(524)	22,874	(436)	22,438	(1,068)	21,370	(1,277)	20,093
TOTAL Public and Indian Housing	3,299,682	34,143	3,333,825	(10,921)	3,322,904	(4,161)	3,318,743	19,820	3,338,563
HOME Tenant Based Rental Assistance[15] (old method)	21,508	(480)	21,028	(4,576)	NA	NA	NA	NA	NA
HOME Tenant Based Rental Assistance[16] (new method)	NA	NA	NA	NA	1,394	0	1,394	0	1,394
HOME Rental	228,613	28,969	257,582	17,674	275,256	20,000	295,256	14,750	310,006
Housing Opportunities for Persons Living With AIDS	25,656	50	25,706	(672)	25,034	(346)	24,688	(76)	24,612
Homeless Assistance Grants	114,763	5,154	119,917	5,647	125,564	5,019	130,583	5,077	135,660
Neighborhood Stabilization Program	3,270	5,388	8,658	6,155	14,813	0	14,813	0	14,813
Tax Credit Assistance Program	14,968	28,298	43,266	16,233	59,499	0	59,499	0	59,499
Gulf Coast (Disaster)	16,969	5,474	22,443	6,598	29,041	TBD	29,041	TBD	29,041
TOTAL Community Planning and Development	427,328	71,272	498,600	47,059	530,601	24,673	555,274	19,751	575,025
HUD TOTAL	5,340,320	107,179	5,447,499	35,534	5,467,975	48,645	5,516,620	73,300	5,589,920

9 Indian Housing Block Grants, PIH Mainstream and Tenant Based Rental Assistance, Multifamily Project Based Rental Assistance, Section 232, TCAP, HOME TBRA, NSP, and Gulf Coast (Disaster) numbers reflect changes from prior reports due to grantee reporting updates.

10 Multifamily Project Based Rental Assistance includes Section 8, Rent Supplement, and Rental Housing Assistance Programs.

11 Other Multifamily Subsidies includes Old Section 202, Section 221(d)(3) Below Market Interest Rate, and Section 236 Interest Reduction Payment only.

12 The notable increase in this target is caused by the addition of renewals with at least 15 years of affordability remaining.

13 Units reported here for the Section 232 program include only units added since the beginning of FY12, when the program was added to this goal.

14 Public Housing FY 2010 baseline is from December 31, 2010. The FY 2011 result is over a performance period of Q2-Q4.

15 Beginning in FY14, HUD is adopting a new methodology for counting assisted households in the HOME TBRA program. In FY10-13, it was assumed that all households assisted received assistance for the maximum two years allowed. Since many households receive more short-term help, HUD will henceforth assume households are only assisted within the quarter of their initial assistance. This requires an adjustment of the FY13 baseline for tracking future results.

16 Ibid.

Additional Data: Rental Assistance Demonstration, Estimated Impacts in FY 2014 and FY 2015

In 2014 and 2015, the Rental Assistance Demonstration (RAD) program will convert assisted rental units from Public Housing, Mod Rehab, Rent Supplement, and Rental Housing Assistance Payment (RAP) programs to Project-Based Rental Assistance (PBRA) or Project-Based Vouchers under the Tenant-Based Rental Assistance program. The chart below shows projected RAD conversions and their impact on the various program categories. Please note that the numbers below reflect total units, not occupied units. The numbers in the charts above and below assume a 95% occupancy rate for all RAD converted units.

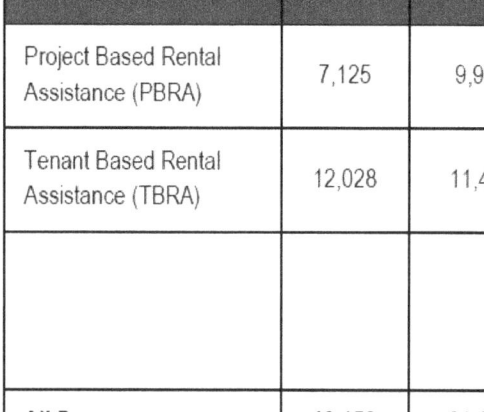

RAD Conversions from:	FY 2014	FY 2015
Public Housing	14,084	19,585
Mod Rehab	166	365
Rent Supplement + Rental Housing Assistance Program (RAP)	4,903	1,425
All Programs:	19,153	21,375

RAD Conversions to:	FY 2014	FY 2015
Project Based Rental Assistance (PBRA)	7,125	9,975
Tenant Based Rental Assistance (TBRA)	12,028	11,400
All Programs:	19,153	21,375

FINAL PROGRESS UPDATE

HUD exceeded its two-year target of 61,000 additional households served by 133 percent, providing affordable rental housing to 142,713 additional households since the beginning of 2012.

For Public and Indian Housing (PIH) programs, flat or reduced program funding was a fundamental challenge in FY13. Public Housing Authorities and Tribally-Designated Housing Entities focused on preservation to ensure currently assisted families could continue to receive housing assistance. For example, the Housing Choice Voucher program faced unprecedented cuts to the administrative fees account in 2012 and 2013, which impacted PHAs' ability to continue to lease units quickly throughout the year. The timing of the passage of the Appropriations Act and the uncertainty of the renewal funding amount was another important factor impacting the Housing Choice Voucher (HCV) program's ability to forecast leasing and achieve leasing goals. Late appropriations or concerns about significant funding reductions cause PHAs to slow or stop leasing to alleviate the number of terminations that may be necessary if drastic reductions in renewal funding materialize. Though these challenges led to reductions in households assisted in public housing and voucher programs in 2013, stronger performance in 2012 enabled PIH to exceed its two-year goals.

Collectively, Community Planning and Development (CPD) programs exceeded their two-year goal by nearly 20,000 units, largely due to rental housing activities in the HOME program. Two programs funded by the American Recovery and Reinvestment Act, the Tax-Credit Assistance Program and the second round of the Neighborhood Stabilization Program (NSP2), were completed in FY13.

HUD continues to work with Treasury and the USDA's Rural Housing Service to align administrative requirements among our respective affordable rental housing programs. This is critical for owners, developers, tenants and local communities working to create and preserve affordable housing as federal funds often make up a significant share of a property's financing structure, and often include overlapping administrative requirements. HUD is collaborating with USDA and Treasury to launch a series of pilots that will streamline administration of our rental programs which we hope will reduce administrative costs associated with these programs over time. In addition, such efforts will increase the effectiveness of HUD's preservation strategies and expand housing opportunities by enabling more voucher holders to access LIHTC units in non-poor neighborhoods.

For detailed quarterly assessments of progress, readers may consult the quarterly updates on Performance.gov.

Strategic Goal 3: Use housing as a platform for improving quality of life

Stable housing, made possible with HUD support, provides an ideal platform for delivering a wide variety of health and social services. Through interagency partnerships at the federal, state, and local levels, HUD will use housing as a platform for coordinating access to a wide variety of services to lower health care costs, end homelessness, and support community living. In additional to the moral imperative to end human suffering caused by homelessness, there are compelling economic reasons for investing in efforts to eradicate this complex social problem. To achieve this goal, HUD will continue to partner with local, state, and federal organizations, including the U.S. Interagency Council on Homelessness, to deploy evidence-based interventions, such as supportive housing, housing first, and rapid rehousing, to more effectively and efficiently use the nation's limited resources to bring an end to homelessness.

▸ **Strategic Objective 3A:** End homelessness for Veterans, people experiencing chronic homelessness, families, youth, and children

▸ **Strategic Objective 3B:** Promote advancements in economic prosperity for residents of HUD-assisted housing

▸ **Strategic Objective 3C:** Promote the health and housing stability of vulnerable populations

Strategic Objective 3A: Homelessness

End homelessness for Veterans, people experiencing chronic homelessness, families, youth, and children.

HUD's annual 'point-in-time' estimates measure the scope of homelessness on a single night in January of each year. Based on data reported by more than 3,000 cities and counties, the January 2013 one-night estimate reveals a 24 percent drop in homelessness among Veterans and a 16 percent reduction among individuals experiencing long-term or chronic homelessness since 2010. HUD's estimate also found the largest decline in the number of persons in families experiencing homelessness since the Department began measuring homelessness in a standard manner in 2005. Overall, a total of 610,042 people experienced homelessness in the United States on a single night in January 2013.

Homelessness among unaccompanied youth is a hidden problem, which HUD and its partners are taking steps to solve. Some subpopulations of youth are at particularly high risk for homelessness, including youth aging out of foster care and LGBTQ youth.

In 2010, the Obama administration released *Opening Doors*[17], the first-ever comprehensive federal strategic plan to prevent and end homelessness. The goals of the plan are to prevent and end Veterans and chronic homelessness by 2015, to prevent and end homelessness for families, youth, and children by 2020, and to set a path to ending all types of homelessness. HUD remains committed to the goals of *Opening Doors*, but to reach them, the pace of current efforts must accelerate. Over the next five years, HUD will work with its partners to deploy the solutions that we know are effective for the right persons, such as rapid re-housing and permanent supportive housing. These tools must be informed by a Housing First approach, where preconditions and barriers to housing entry are removed and people move into housing as quickly as possible.

STRATEGIES

- **Implement the Homelessness Emergency and Rapid Transition to Housing (HEARTH) Act** with a focus on technical assistance for prioritized access to housing and use of community data to manage performance. This includes encouraging Continuums of Care to use their existing resources more effectively. In particular, CoCs are encouraged to use reallocation of existing projects in favor of creating new permanent supportive housing for the chronically homeless or rapid re housing for homeless households with children that are coming from the streets or shelters, as well as prioritizing the chronically homeless and those whose needs are most acute in all existing permanent supportive housing.

- **Fully engage and leverage mainstream housing assistance,** including housing choice vouchers, public housing, HOME Investment Partnerships and Community Development Block Grants, and

---

[17] United States Interagency Council on Homelessness, *Opening Doors: Federal Strategic Plan to Prevent and End Homelessness* (June 2010).

multifamily housing. We will build capacity among public housing authorities and multifamily owners to admit homeless households into their units and provide them with vouchers.

- **Improve data and performance management** through strategies to share data across systems, adoption of a common data standard for housing stability, and use of Homeless Management Information Systems (HMIS) by homeless programs funded by the Department of Veterans Affairs (VA) and the Department of Health and Human Services (HHS).

- **Continue to strengthen collaborations** at all levels of government and with the private sector, including within HUD, and with the US Interagency Council on Homelessness (USICH), the VA, HHS, the Department of Labor, the Department of Education, the Department of Agriculture, and others.

- **Implement USICH Framework to End Youth Homelessness,** including integrating HMIS and Runaway and Homeless Youth Management Information systems, leveraging HUD's Point-in-Time count to improve strategies for counting youth, and developing a national study that builds on program data and the HUD count that includes household surveys to get to a confident national estimate of youth homelessness.

- **Promote implementation of coordinated assessment systems for Continuums of Care** through training, technical assistance and guidance by the Office of Special Needs Assistance Programs to better target resources.

LEADING THIS OBJECTIVE

Jennifer Ho, *Senior Advisor on Housing and Services*, Office of the Secretary

MAJOR MILESTONES

9/30/2014   **Implement PIT count improvements for youth**

Implement more accurate Point-In-Time (PIT) count of youth experiencing homelessness through improved PIT guidance for 2014 and 2015 PIT counts, based on findings from YouthCount!

10/1/2014   **Integrate RHYMIS and HMIS**

In partnership with HHS, integrate RHYMIS (Runaway and Homeless Youth Management Information System) and HMIS (Homeless Management Information System) to improve data collection and facilitate interagency efforts to end youth homelessness.

10/1/2015   **Data improvements for chronic homelessness**

Improve data quality on persons experiencing chronic homelessness through implementing additional data elements in the HMIS data standards, additional fields on chronic status in the Annual Performance Report (APR), and additional fields in the CoC competition application form on Permanent Supportive Housing beds prioritized for persons experiencing chronic homelessness.

1/1/2016   **Implement PIT count improvements for veterans**

In partnership with VA, improve the methodology and reporting of Veterans homelessness through the annual PIT count to acquire timely, reliable, and detailed data regarding the number of homeless veterans.

To track our progress towards this objective, HUD will monitor completion of the following performance indicators.

○ <u>Fiscal Year 2014-2015 Agency Priority Goal</u>:

In partnership, the Department of Housing and Urban Development and the Department of Veteran Affairs (VA) aim to reduce the number of Veterans living on the streets, experiencing homelessness to zero (as measured by the 2016 Point-in-Time count).

▶ ○ **Total homeless Veterans temporarily living in shelters or transitional housing** (key measure)
This metric will be measured by the annual <u>Point-in-Time count</u>, a count of homeless persons on a single night in January each year.

FY11 Actual	FY12 Actual	FY13 Actual	FY14 Target	FY15 Target
35,143	34,695	No Data[18]	23,500	12,500

▶ ○ **Total Veterans living on the streets, experiencing homelessness** (key measure)
This metric will be measured by the annual <u>Point-in-Time count</u>, a count of homeless persons on a single night in January each year.

FY11 Actual	FY12 Actual	FY13 Actual	FY14 Target	FY15 Target
27,476	23,368	No Data[19]	4,000	0

▶ ○ **Veterans placed in permanent housing** (supporting measure shared by VA and HUD)
This includes moves into HUD–Veterans Affairs Supportive Housing (HUD-VASH) Program, rapid rehousing placements through Supportive Services for Veteran Families (SSVF) program, and moves from VA residential treatment programs into permanent housing.

FY11 Actual	FY12 Actual	FY13 Actual	FY14 Target	FY15 Target
NA	NA	TBD	40,000	Target TBD

▶ ○ **Homeless Veterans served with transitional housing through Continuum of Care resources** (supporting measure; HUD only)

FY11 Actual	FY12 Actual	FY13 Actual	FY14 Target	FY15 Target
8,443	10,734	TBD	9,661	9,178

---

[18] A full calculation of HUD's impact on reducing homelessness by the end of FY 2013 will be assessed during final analysis of results from the annual Point-In-Time (PIT) count of the homeless population throughout the nation, which took place on a single night in January 2014.
[19] Ibid.

▶ ✪ **Homeless Veterans served with permanent supportive housing through Continuum of Care resources** (supporting measure: HUD only)

FY11 Actual	FY12 Actual	FY13 Actual	FY14 Target	FY15 Target
6,982	11,962	NA	12,360	12,731

<u>Other Measures:</u>

▸ **Individuals experiencing chronic homelessness**

FY11 Actual	FY12 Actual	FY13 Actual	FY14 Target	FY15 Target
99,894	92,593	No Data[20]	80,500	66,000

▸ **Number of new Permanent Supportive Housing beds dedicated[21] to individuals and families experiencing chronic homelessness**

FY11 Actual	FY12 Actual	FY13 Actual	FY14 Target	FY15 Target
4,315	1,932	No Data	4,530	37,000

▸ **Percentage of new Permanent Supportive Housing beds dedicated to individuals and families experiencing chronic homelessness**

FY11 Actual	FY12 Actual	FY13 Actual	FY14 Target	FY15 Target
50.0%	36.9%	No Data	100%	100%

▸ **Percentage of Permanent Supportive Housing beds targeted to individuals experiencing chronic homelessness**

FY11 Actual	FY12 Actual	FY13 Actual	FY14 Target	FY15 Target
NA	NA	NA	43.0%	44.0%

▸ **Families experiencing homelessness**

FY11 Actual	FY12 Actual	FY13 Actual	FY14 Target	FY15 Target
77,157	70,960	No Data[22]	Establish Baseline	Target TBD

▸ **Admissions of new homeless families into HUD-assisted Housing (Public Housing and Housing Choice Vouchers)**

FY11 Actual	FY12 Actual	FY13 Actual	FY14 Target	FY15 Target
No Data	5,674	11,452	Establish Baseline	Target TBD

▸ **Admissions of new homeless families into HUD-assisted Housing (Multifamily)**

FY11 Actual	FY12 Actual	FY13 Actual	FY14 Target	FY15 Target
No Data	No Data	No Data	Establish Baseline	Target TBD

---

[20] Ibid.

[21] The term *dedicated beds* means that the provider is obligated by contract or otherwise to serve chronically homeless persons and when a participant exits the program, the bed must be filled by another chronically homeless participant unless there are no chronically homeless persons located within the geographic area. A bed is *prioritized* for chronically homeless persons when a participant exits the program and eligible chronically homeless persons are offered the bed before any other population. The term *targeted* means the sum of dedicated and prioritized beds.

[22] Ibid.

▶ Percentage of Emergency Solutions Grant dollars dedicated to Rapid Rehousing for homeless families

FY11 Actual	FY12 Actual	FY13 Actual	FY14 Target	FY15 Target
NA	NA	NA	Establish Baseline	Target TBD

Retrospective: FY 2012-2013 Agency Priority Goal · Veterans' Homelessness

Between October 1, 2011 and September 30, 2013, HUD aimed to reduce the number of homeless Veterans to 35,000 by serving 35,500 additional homeless Veterans. By the close of FY 2013, HUD, in partnership with the VA, had served 46,153 Veterans, surpassing—by over 10,000—its two-year goal. HUD continues to work toward its goal of a reduction in Veterans' homelessness to 35,000 individuals, and based on the annual Point-in-Time count in January 2013, the number of homeless Veterans has decreased by 24% since 2010.

	Target	Actual	Change from Previous Year (%)	Target Met?

Homeless Veterans assisted by HUD programs

This measure combines the totals of Veterans assisted through HUD's program-specific measures for Veterans served by HUD-Veterans Affairs Supportive Housing (HUD-VASH), the Continuum of Care (CoC) Permanent Supportive Housing Programs, and the Homelessness Prevention and Rapid Rehousing (HPRP).

	Target	Actual	Change from Previous Year (%)	Target Met?
2010		26,578		
2011		32,652	+6,074 (↑23%)	
2012	19,678	31,487	-1,165 (↓4%)	✓
2013	16,057	14,666[23]	TBA	TBA
2012+2013	35,735	46,153[24]	TBA	✓
		net change, 2010 – 2013	+105,383 Vets housed	

HUD-VASH Veterans assisted

This measure tracks the number of Veterans assisted by the HUD-Veterans Affairs Supportive Housing (HUD-VASH) program, which combines Housing Choice Voucher rental assistance for homeless Veterans with case management and clinical services provided by the Department of Veterans Affairs (VA).

	Target	Actual	Change from Previous Year (%)	Target Met?
2010		11,140		
2011		14,621	+3,481 (↑31%)	
2012	12,200	15,450	+829 (↑6%)	✓
2013	12,200	14,666	-784 (↓5%)	✓

Veterans who are homeless or at risk of homelessness assisted with HPRP funds

This measure tracks the number of homeless Veterans who either are homeless or are at risk of becoming homeless and who are served through the Homelessness Prevention and Rapid Rehousing Program (HPRP), which was funded through the Recovery Act.

	Target	Actual	Change from Previous Year (%)	Target Met?
2010		11,385		
2011		11,049	-336 (↓3%)	
2012	3,750	4,075	-6,974 (-63%)	✓
2013	0	NA	NA	

---

[23] Does not yet include a 2013 count of the number of homeless Veterans served through Continuum of Care permanent supportive housing programs.

[24] Ibid.

Homeless Veterans served through Continuum of Care permanent supportive housing programs

This indicator will come from the annual Point-in-Time Count.

2010		4,053		
2011		6,982	2,929 (↑72%)	
2012	3,728	11,962	4,980 (↑71%)	✓
2013	3,857	TBA[25]	TBA	

■ Target   ■ Actual

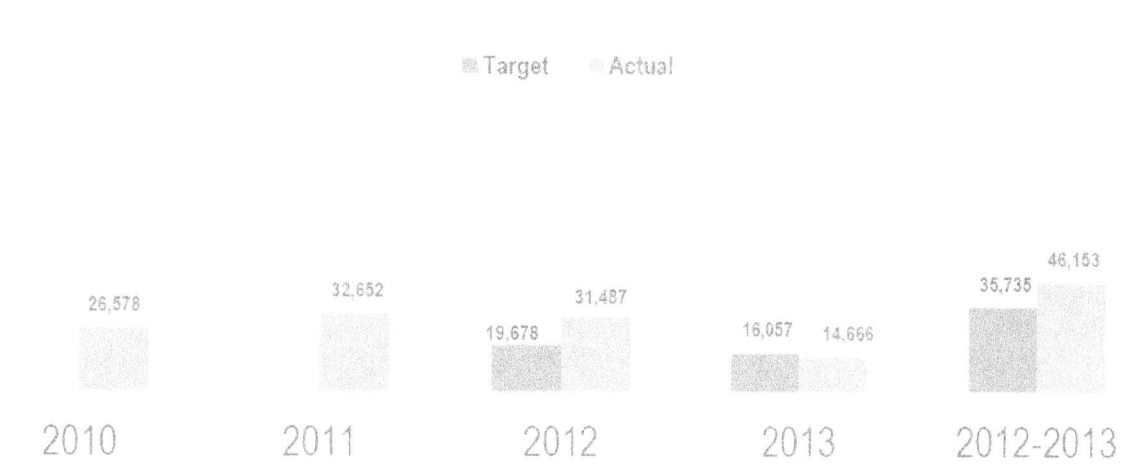

Figure 2 Homeless Veterans assisted by HUD programs, 2010-2013 *(preliminary results)*

---

[25] A full calculation of HUD's impact on reducing homelessness by the end of FY 2013 will be assessed during final analysis of results from the annual Point-In-Time (PIT) count of the homeless population throughout the nation, which took place on a single night in January 2014.

FY 2012-2013 Agency Priority Goal ▪ Veterans' Homelessness

Between October 1, 2011 and September 30, 2013, HUD aimed to reduce the number of homeless Veterans to 35,000 by serving 35,500 additional homeless Veterans. By the close of FY 2013, HUD, in partnership with the VA, had served 46,153 Veterans, surpassing—by 10,418—its two-year goal of serving 35,735 Veterans. HUD continues to work toward its goal of a reduction in Veterans' homelessness to 35,000 individuals, and based on the annual Point-in-Time count in January 2013, the number of homeless Veterans has decreased by 24% since 2010.

Through the end of FY 2013, HUD-VASH program targets for serving homeless Veterans were exceeded by 23 percent, with participating Public Housing Authorities (PHAs) serving 30,116 homeless Veterans. In FY 2012 alone, 11,962 Veterans were served by Continuum of Care funded Permanent Supportive Housing programs, exceeding the combined FY12-13 target by 58 percent. Also in FY 2012, 4,075 Veterans were served by Homeless Prevention and Rapid Rehousing (HPRP) dollars, exceeding combined the FY12-13 target by 9%. Readers may continue to track HUD's progress on this priority goal by viewing quarterly updates on Performance.gov.

In order to meet the goal of ending Veteran's homelessness by 2015, HUD and the Department of Veterans Affairs have worked diligently to target HUD-VASH vouchers and supportive services to chronically homeless Veterans. The HUD-VASH program is jointly administered in communities by VA Medical Center (VAMC) and Public Housing Authority (PHA) staff, with help from Continuums of Care and other local partners. HUD and the VA participate in ongoing planning meetings to ensure that communications and strategies for the two agencies remain open and aligned. As part of their continued commitment to joint problem solving and improvement of efforts, HUD and VA jointly committed to pursuing a short-term goal of facilitating more effective information sharing between Continuums of Care and VA Medical Centers about the homeless Veterans they serve.

For detailed quarterly assessments of progress on this goal, readers may consult the quarterly updates on Performance.gov.

Strategic Objective 3B: Economic Prosperity

Promote advancements in economic prosperity for residents of HUD-assisted housing

OVERVIEW

Residents of HUD-assisted housing often face challenges such as lack of employable skills and low educational attainment levels that limit their ability to become economically self-sufficient and rise out of poverty. The Department recognizes that while some families and individuals will need assistance for longer periods, others are capable, with assistance, of rising out of poverty. A majority of adults receiving rental assistance who are able to work have some income from wages; however, they are most often in the lowest-paying jobs. Further, increasing workplace demands for technical expertise require attention to education and training for both adults and youth, including digital literacy. HUD will utilize its housing platform to expand access to employment and educational services. HUD seeks to significantly increase the economic opportunities available to low-income residents in neighborhoods where it invests, particularly through the Family Self Sufficiency (FSS) program and Section 3[26].

STRATEGIES

- **Build evidence on effectiveness of programs that promote economic self-sufficiency** by evaluating the FSS program through a randomized controlled trial by 2018.

- **Implement an evidence-based evaluation to improve reentry outcomes for formerly incarcerated individuals and their communities.** HUD will assess models that deliver permanent supportive housing linked with employment, behavioral health services, and family unification. HUD is considering options ranging from an evaluation of existing PHA reentry programs to an interagency effort that would involve leveraging private/philanthropic investments to support permanent supportive housing plus services within a pay-for-success framework.

- **Expand the Section 3 Business Registry system nationwide.** A five city pilot, started in in FY 2012 in Detroit, Miami, New Orleans, Los Angeles, and Washington, DC, provides recipients of HUD funding with access to a registry of self-certified local Section 3 businesses and has demonstrated promising results in increasing contracts awarded to Section 3 businesses. Expanding the registry nationwide will be supported with training, HUD guidance, and marketing to increase awareness of this resource.

- **Strengthen collaboration between HUD programs to ensure recipients have adequate guidance and technical assistance and that HUD has a coordinated approach to compliance.** Section 3 compliance is overseen by HUD's Office of Fair Housing and Equal Opportunity, but funding is distributed to recipients through other program offices, including the Office of Public and Indian Housing,

---

[26] <u>Section 3</u> of the Housing and Urban Development Act of 1968 requires that recipients of certain HUD financial assistance, to the greatest extent feasible, provide job training, employment, and contracting opportunities for low- or very-low income residents in connection with projects and activities in their neighborhoods and to the businesses that substantially employ them.

the Office of Community Planning and Development, the Office of Housing, and the Office of Lead Hazard Control and Healthy Homes. Increased coordination, both by providing technical assistance and resolving compliance issues, will increase the impact that Section 3 has on communities and be responsive to the Office of Inspector General audit findings.

LEADING THIS OBJECTIVE

Janet Hostetler, *Senior Advisor* for the Office of Fair Housing and Equal Opportunity

Dominique Blom, *Deputy Assistant Secretary*, Office of Public Housing Investments

MAJOR MILESTONES

6/30/2014	**Release new Section 3 reporting tool for funding recipients.**
11/30/2014	**Release proposed Section 3 Rule.**
2/28/2015	**Collect baseline data on Section 3 results** using new Section 3 reporting tool.
2/28/2015	**Implement the Jobs Plus program** to enhance and measure impact of the place-based employment and asset-building model.
9/30/2015	**Assess current capacity of Neighborhood Network Centers** in Multi-family and public housing developments to improve residents' digital literacy and access to online resources.
11/30/2015	**Release final Section 3 Rule,** and provide guidance and TA on new rule.

MEASURING OUR PROGRESS

To track our progress towards this objective, HUD will monitor the following performance indicators.

▶ **Percentage of participants enrolled in the Family Self Sufficiency program that have increased wages**

FY11 Actual	FY12 Actual[27]	CY13 Actual	FY14 Target	FY15 Target
58%	58%[28]	53%[29]	Establish Baseline	Target TBD

---

[27] For the purposes of this particular measure, which is new, the measurement period was 4/1/11 – 3/30/12, rather than full fiscal year 2012.

[28] As of March 30, 2012, a total of 57,087 families were enrolled in the HCV and PH FSS programs (47,888 in HCV FSS and 9,199 in PH FSS).

[29] Note this is for Calendar Year 2013, rather than Fiscal Year 2013. Further analysis of this measure shows that 41% of Public Housing FSS continuing participants, 48% of Public Housing FSS graduates, 56% of Housing Choice Voucher FSS continuing participants, and 54% of Housing Choice Voucher FSS graduates reported increased wages.

Section 3 of the Housing and Urban Development Act of 1968 requires that recipients of certain HUD financial assistance, to the greatest extent feasible, provide job training, employment, and contracting opportunities for low- or very-low income residents in connection with projects and activities in their neighborhoods and to the businesses that substantially employ them.

▶ **Percentage of Section 3 residents hired, of total hiring that occurs as a result of Section 3 covered HUD funding**
Note: The regulatory target for Section 3 residents hired is 30% of total hiring.

FY11 Actual	FY12 Actual	FY13 Actual	FY14 Target	FY15 Target
36.8%	44.1%	TBD	45.0%	45.0%

▶ **Percentage of total dollar amount of construction contracts awarded to Section 3 businesses by covered HUD funding**
Note: The regulatory target for Section 3 business construction contracts is 10 percent of the total dollar amount of construction contracts.

FY11 Actual	FY12 Actual	FY13 Actual	FY14 Target	FY15 Target
9.5%	7.1%	TBD	9.5%	9.75%

▶ **Percentage of total dollar amount of non-construction contracts awarded to Section 3 businesses by covered HUD funding**
Note: The regulatory target for Section 3 business non-construction contracts is 3 percent of the total dollar amount of non-construction contracts.

FY11 Actual	FY12 Actual	FY13 Actual	FY14 Target	FY15 Target
1.9%	3.4%	TBD	3.5%	3.5%

▶ **Percentage of HUD funding recipients that used HUD money to hire staff and execute construction and non-construction contracts that met all three numerical goals[30]**

FY11 Actual	FY12 Actual	FY13 Actual	FY14 Target	FY15 Target
11.8%	13.2%	TBD	13.5%	13.75%

▶ **Number of self-certified Section 3 businesses in HUD's registry nationwide**
The Section 3 business registry is expected to be released nationwide in September 2014. The first year of nationwide operation will be used to develop baseline data. Targets will depend on creating this baseline data.

FY11 Actual	FY12 Actual	FY13 Actual	FY14 Target	FY15 Target
NA	NA	NA	NA	Target TBD

---

[30] In HUD's recently published Strategic Plan 2014-2018, the Department intended to measure the percentage of Section 3 covered funding recipients who timely meet reporting, hiring, and contracting requirements. However, based on lack of data availability for that precise metric, a closely related metric has been substituted: the percentage of HUD funding recipients that used HUD money to hire staff and execute construction and non-construction contracts that met all three numerical goals.

Strategic Objective 3C: Health and Housing Stability

Promote the health and housing stability of vulnerable populations.

OVERVIEW

Many residents of HUD-assisted housing face health-related challenges, especially the elderly, people with disabilities, homeless people, and those individuals and families at risk of becoming homeless. New studies of the health status of HUD residents show that they have higher rates of chronic health conditions and higher utilization of hospitals and emergency rooms than peer comparison groups. Some may have a criminal record, a history of homelessness, be making the transition out of military service back into civilian life, or be transitioning out of health care treatment settings.

In 2013, one out of every six Americans did not have health insurance. Hardworking families in HUD housing may not get insurance from their employers, and they may not make enough money to afford a plan for their family. Without health insurance, families risk forgoing necessary preventive care or facing economic catastrophe from a major illness.

In January 2014, many more affordable insurance options became available through the new health insurance marketplaces, including, in those states that have opted in, an expansion of Medicaid. When residents of HUD-assisted housing also have health insurance, they gain an additional stepping stone to better health and financial security. This makes for healthier, stronger households and communities.

The Affordable Care Act can help as many as 40 million currently uninsured Americans find greater peace of mind and financial stability that will help them work toward their own goals and dreams. Access to health insurance is important, but so too is access to health care. As the health care system develops new tools to provide better care at a lower cost, new partnerships are needed between housing and the health care system.

Additionally, work led by DOJ and HHS related to enforcement of and compliance with the Supreme Court's *Olmstead* decision[31] reinforces the rights of individuals with disabilities to live, work, and receive services in the greater community in the most integrated setting appropriate to their needs. As a result of Olmstead, there is a significant need for affordable, integrated housing opportunities where individuals with disabilities are able to live and interact with individuals without disabilities. Achieving this goal requires an increase in the supply of integrated housing options so that individuals have meaningful choice in where they live, including housing without services and supportive housing with access to voluntary services.

---

[31] Olmstead v. L.C., 57 U.S. 581 (1999)

HUD also helps protect the health of residents of assisted multifamily and public housing from both direct and environmental (i.e., second-hand and third-hand) tobacco smoke exposure by encouraging owners of assisted housing, and public housing agencies to issue and implement smoke free policies, and by providing outreach and technical support. The Department will enhance those efforts to help reduce the extent of this public health problem among residents of its housing portfolio.

STRATEGIES

- **Promote health and financial stability of vulnerable populations by identifying opportunities to determine eligibility for Medicaid automatically or routinely.** HUD will use income information collected in HUD funded programs and partner with state Medicaid programs and health insurance navigators.

- **Build evidence on effective models for coupling services with housing** and modify existing and future programs to reflect best practices

- **Improve performance management by enhancing HUD's collection and analysis of data** pertaining to health-related outcomes across HUD-assisted housing programs. Also improve HUD's ability to integrate and/or conduct administrative data matches with other partner federal programs.

- **Assist with enforcement and implementation of the Supreme Court's Olmstead decision,** in collaboration with HHS, DOJ, and state agencies, through facilitating expansion of integrated housing opportunities for people with disabilities transitioning out of institutions/at risk of institutionalization, including people experiencing homelessness.

- **Increase the number of public housing agencies that have issued smoke-free policies.** In accordance with recommendations by the Surgeon General,[32,33] and the systematic review by the Department of Health and Human Services-chartered Task Force on Community Preventive Services on the effectiveness of smoke-free policies,[34] the public health of residents of public housing, both smokers and non-smokers, is improved when the management issues and implements a smoke free policy. Research by the Centers for Disease Control and Prevention indicates that such policies in assisted housing are associated with cost savings.[35] HUD will expand its encouragement of such policies through notices, guidance, outreach and technical support, and track the issuance and implementation of smoke free policies by public housing agencies.

---

[32] The Health Consequences of Smoking—50 Years of Progress: A Report of the Surgeon General, 2014; www.surgeongeneral.gov/library/reports/50-years-of-progress/index.html

[33] Reducing Tobacco Use. A Report of the Surgeon General, 2000; www.cdc.gov/tobacco/data_statistics/sgr/2000/index.htm

[34] Task Force on Community Preventive Services. The Guide to Community Preventive Services: What Works to Promote Health?, 2005; www.thecommunityguide.org/tobacco/Tobacco.pdf

[35] King BA, Peck RM, Babb SD. Cost Savings Associated with Prohibiting Smoking in U.S. Subsidized Housing. Am J Prev Med. 2013 Jun;44(6):631-4; www.ncbi.nlm.nih.gov/pubmed/23683981

LEADING THIS OBJECTIVE

Jennifer Ho, *Senior Advisor on Housing and Services*, Office of the Secretary

MAJOR MILESTONES

7/30/2014   **Publish interim report for evaluation of SASH in Vermont**
In partnership with the HHS Office of Assistant Secretary for Planning and
Evaluation (ASPE), complete evaluation of Supports and Services at Home
(SASH) program in Vermont

12/31/2014   **Complete CMS data matching of HUD-assisted seniors**
With the Center for Medicare and Medicaid Services (CMS), complete data
matching of seniors living in a range of HUD-assisted housing in 12 jurisdictions to
their Medicare claims records to assess health care utilization, expenditures, and
diagnoses.

9/30/2015   **Initiate Demonstration of Age in Place Pilot**
Collaborate with the Center for Medicare and Medicaid Services and HHS to
develop and implement a pilot or demonstration that delivers housing and service
to support older residents of federally assisted housing to age in place and to
determine resident outcomes and cost savings

MEASURING OUR PROGRESS

To track our progress towards this objective, HUD will monitor the following performance indicators.

▶ **Number of successful transitions from institutions through Section 811 Project Rental Assistance program**

FY11 Actual	FY12 Actual	FY13 Actual	FY14 Target	FY15 Target
No data	No data	No data	Establish Baseline	Target TBD

▶ **Percentage of HUD-assisted residents with public or private health coverage (Source: National Health Interview Survey)**

FY11 Actual	FY12 Actual	FY13 Actual	FY14 Target	FY15 Target
No data	No data	No data[36]	Establish Baseline	Target TBD

▶ **Number of PHAs with smoke-free housing policies (cumulative)[37]**

CY11 Actual	CY12 Actual	CY13 Actual	FY14 Target	FY15 Target
10%	13%	15%	16%	19%

---

[36] Data are not available. The National Center for Health Statistics is currently engaged in the data matching
work necessary to finalize data for this metric.

[37] Some historical data on smoke-free public housing policies relies on data compiled by state public health
departments or other state/regional sources. These data sources did not always identify when a policy was put in
place. For purposes of inclusion in this historical data table, all of the PHAs with unknown dates of adoption (83
PHAs) are recorded in the CY 2011 total. This approach is appropriately conservative in ensuring we are not
overestimating more recent progress.

Goal 4: Build Strong, Resilient, and Inclusive Communities

Housing and community development efforts must address a complex network of individual, social, economic, and environmental factors in order to promote more diverse, inclusive communities and improve the sustainability of neighborhoods, communities, and regions. Many of the neighborhoods hit hardest by the housing and economic crisis—those with the highest rates of foreclosure and job loss—have been racially isolated and among the least sustainable, with limited access to economic opportunity, the longest commuting times to jobs, the most homes that pose health risks, and the poorest quality schools.

It is crucial that the federal government and its local partners effectively coordinate policies related to community development, climate change, energy efficiency, transportation, and disaster preparedness. Today we know that "place" influences outcomes—the place where a person lives is a reliable predictor of his or her long-term health, education, and employment outcomes. Families and individuals living in concentrated poverty experience greater inequity and often, as a result, more dismal outcomes.

Residents of these neighborhoods have limited access to transportation, face health hazards in their home and communities, suffer from the poorest schools, and have the fewest economic opportunities. In many areas, the spatial mismatch between housing and transportation investments limits access to decent employment and education opportunities for entire neighborhoods. This not only impacts the lives of residents in those communities, but the resulting need to travel greater distances to connect to these resources has a clear impact on the environment as well—from wetland and open space lost to sprawling development patterns to ever increasing greenhouse gas emissions.

To address these problems, Goal 4 focuses explicitly on "place," on preparing communities for the future of their economy, environment, and community development, through enhanced planning, enforcement, and capacity building—so that all communities are livable for residents and viable in the long-term.

The following strategic objectives provide a roadmap for accomplishing this goal:

▸ **Strategic Objective 4A:** Reduce housing discrimination, affirmatively further fair housing through HUD programs, and promote diverse, inclusive communities

▸ **Strategic Objective 4B:** Increase the health and safety of homes and embed comprehensive energy efficiency and healthy housing criteria across HUD programs

▸ **Strategic Objective 4C:** Support the recovery of communities from disasters by promoting community resilience, developing state and local capacity, and ensuring a coordinated federal response that reduces risk and produces a more resilient built environment

▸ **Strategic Objective 4D:** Strengthen communities' economic health, resilience and access to opportunity

Strategic Objective 4A: Fair Housing

Reduce housing discrimination, affirmatively further fair housing through HUD programs, and promote diverse, inclusive communities.

OVERVIEW

HUD seeks to significantly increase the number of housing providers, lenders, members of the real estate community, and others that fully comply with the Fair Housing Act and other applicable fair housing and civil rights laws and do not discriminate on any basis prohibited by those laws and regulations. While housing discrimination still takes on blatant forms in some instances, it has become more subtle and sophisticated through the years, resulting in underreporting and complicating effective enforcement.

In addition to enforcement, HUD works proactively to make access to important neighborhood assets measurably fairer, to significantly increase the economic opportunities available to low-income residents in neighborhoods where HUD invests, and to ensure that policies and practices are in place to provide equal access to persons with disabilities.

STRATEGIES

- **Ensure compliance with civil rights and economic opportunity requirements by providing high-quality technical assistance and training to stakeholders.** Over the coming four years, HUD will provide technical assistance on fair housing and civil rights laws and program requirements, such as the obligation to affirmatively further fair housing (AFFH), Section 3, Title VI, Section 504, and other areas of civil rights compliance so that HUD grantees have enough information and guidance to comply with civil rights requirements. This will include increasing technical assistance on fair housing issues and more effectively embedding civil rights requirements into other technical assistance offered by HUD.

- **Reduce discrimination by educating housing providers and by publicizing the consequences of violating the law.** In the coming four years, HUD will target housing providers, lenders, real estate agents, apartment managers and others that work in the housing industry for training and outreach to educate them on their responsibilities under the Fair Housing Act and other applicable fair housing and civil rights laws, in order to improve compliance with those laws. HUD will expand availability of fair housing educational material for industry representatives and consumers through website offerings. HUD will also strategically use press, public engagement, and other education and outreach techniques to deter discrimination.

- **Stop discrimination through strong enforcement of the law against violators**, with a particular focus on systemic cases (those matters involving widespread discrimination affecting multiple people), more meaningful case outcomes, and enforcement strategies that identify and change widespread policies and practices.

LEADING THIS OBJECTIVE

Bryan Greene, *Acting Assistant Secretary*, Office of Fair Housing and Equal Opportunity

MAJOR MILESTONES

TBD	Develop a measure for assessing the effect of targeted education and outreach efforts to those in the housing industry.[38]
1/1/2015	Develop internal expertise throughout HUD on Affirmatively Furthering Fair Housing
9/30/2015	Publish final Affirmatively Furthering Fair Housing regulation
9/30/2015	Develop and publish AFH template, guidance, technical assistance, and standards for program participants under the new regulation (tie to publication of Final Rule)
4/1/2016	Creation of website with consolidated information on fair housing

MEASURING OUR PROGRESS

To track our progress towards this objective, HUD will monitor progress on the following indicators:

- ► Number of people receiving remedies through Fair Housing Act enforcement work

FY11 Actual	FY12 Actual	FY13 Actual	FY14 Target	FY15 Target
1,245	2,043	4,147	Tracking Only	Tracking Only

- ► Number of people receiving remedies through Fair Housing Act enforcement work *per case*

FY11 Actual	FY12 Actual	FY13 Actual	FY14 Target	FY15 Target
1.7	2.3	5.3	Tracking Only	Tracking Only

- ► Monetary relief per case received through Fair Housing Act enforcement work (for cases with relief less than $100,000)

FY11 Actual	FY12 Actual	FY13 Actual	FY14 Target	FY15 Target
$2,154	$2,483	$3,666	Tracking Only	Tracking Only

---

[38] Tentative milestone; proposed by OMB. Not yet approved by FHEO.

Strategic Objective 4B: Green and Healthy Homes

Increase the health and safety of homes and embed comprehensive energy efficiency and healthy housing criteria across HUD programs.

OVERVIEW

HUD has committed to creating energy efficient, green, and healthy housing as part of a broader effort to foster the development of inclusive, sustainable communities. The residential sector is responsible for fully 21 percent of the nation's greenhouse gas emissions. HUD itself spends an estimated $6.4 billion annually on utilities (both water and energy) in the form of allowances for tenant-paid utilities, direct operating grants for public housing, and housing assistance payments for privately-owned assisted housing. Utility costs account for around 22 percent of public housing operating budgets, and a similar share in the assisted housing sector.

Reducing these rising costs – generating savings for residents and owners, as well as for taxpayers – is a key HUD priority. Housing is also an important determinant of health, and poor housing conditions are associated with a wide range of health conditions, including respiratory infections, asthma, lead poisoning, injuries, and other housing-related health hazards. Significant progress has been made over the past four years with completed energy retrofits, healthy housing interventions, or new energy projects in more than 360,000 housing units.

From 2014-2018, HUD aims to continue to focus on energy and health investments in HUD-assisted housing, as well as in market-rate housing, to support the goals of President Obama's Climate Action Plan to cut energy waste in half by 2030 and accelerate clean energy leadership. We will reduce barriers to financing energy efficiency as well as on-site renewable energy, help unlock innovative and traditional sources of capital, and raise the bar on codes and standards that promote energy efficiency and healthy housing.

STRATEGIES

Boost Energy Efficiency and Renewable Energy

- **Strengthen HUD's programs and policies to meet the President's goal of cutting energy waste in half by 2030 in new and existing HUD-assisted housing.** This includes continuing to update energy codes and standards; implementing a green Physical Needs Assessment (PNA) in public housing and an analogous Capital Needs Assessment e-tool in multifamily housing; and supporting the adoption of comprehensive utility benchmarking protocols across HUD's portfolio. This strategy will help HUD stakeholders reduce energy consumption and improve building performance. This will be accomplished through voluntary efforts such as the Better Buildings Challenge, partnerships with DOE, EPA, USDA and other federal agencies, and leveraging HUD's Technical Assistance resources.

- **Implement national partnerships to triple the amount of on-site renewable energy across the federally assisted housing stock by 2020.** This joint effort of HUD, the Department of Agriculture (USDA), and the Treasury Department will for the first time focus on solar and renewable energy in federally-assisted housing, by implementing a key goal of the President's Climate Action Plan, to reach

100 megawatts – equivalent to the energy used by over 30,000 homes[39] – of on-site renewable energy in federally assisted housing.

- **Overcome barriers to leveraging private sector and other innovative sources of capital for energy efficiency and renewable energy investments.** HUD, in concert with other federal and state partners, will help expand the pool of private and public capital investment for energy efficiency and renewable energy programs across the residential spectrum.

Enhance Safe and Healthy Housing

- **Expand housing management practices that protect the health of residents.**

- **Investigate HUD's existing methods to assess the physical condition of assisted housing for potential improvements in identifying defects shown to adversely impact health.**
  HUD's existing physical condition assessment methods focus on traditional physical safety hazards, which may miss certain recognized conditions that can result in health hazards. Consistent with the *Surgeon General's Call to Action to Promote Healthy Homes*,[40] HUD's *Leading Our Nation to Healthier Homes: The Healthy Homes Strategic Plan*,[41] and the federal *Advancing Healthy Housing: A Strategy for Action*,[42] HUD will conduct a review of existing physical condition assessment methods for potential improvements in identifying health hazards. This review will include HUD's physical condition assessment protocols, such as the Uniform Physical Condition Standards for Voucher Programs (UPCS-V).

Strengthen Environmental Reviews

- **Strengthen the environmental review process.** HUD will strengthen the environmental review process to require resilient projects by pursuing rulemaking to require flood mitigation in special flood hazard areas. Furthermore, HUD will ensure that building occupants are safe from hazards, such as radon, through clarification and enforcement of HUD's regulatory requirement that all projects are free of contaminants and hazards that could affect the health and safety of occupants. Finally, through continued support and emphasis on a thorough and complete environmental review, HUD will be supporting safe, sustainable projects that have a minimal negative impact on the environment.

LEADING THIS OBJECTIVE

Trisha Miller, *Senior Advisor*, Office of Economic Resilience

Matthew Ammon, *Acting Director*, Office of Lead Hazard Control and Healthy Homes

---

[39] http://www.eia.gov/consumption/residential/reports/2009/consumption-down.cfm?src=‹%20Consumption-f3

[40] http://www.surgeongeneral.gov/library/calls/healthyhomes/index.html

[41] http://www.hud.gov/offices/lead/library/hhi/hh_strategic_plan.pdf

[42] http://portal.hud.gov/hudportal/HUD?src=/program_offices/healthy_homes/advhh

MAJOR MILESTONES

12/31/2014

Expand the Better Buildings Challenge, with a goal of recruiting 100 Multifamily Partners, Financial Allies, and Utility Partners

Dates vary depending on specific milestone in this category

Update and align energy criteria in funding programs, including code updates yearly or as appropriate

- Publish General Section for FY14 and FY15 NOFA with threshold energy requirements and bonus points
- Publish Preliminary IECC/ASHRAE Determination
- Publish Final IECC/ASHRAE Determination
- Complete HOME Energy Rule

12/31/2015

Utility Data Collection/Roll out Benchmarking to Portfolio

- Launch 1-100 Energy Star score for multifamily residential buildings
- Implement PIH Benchmarking pilot
- Rollout department-wide energy data collection/benchmarking policy for assisted and public housing.

Dates vary depending on specific milestone in this category

Explore innovative financing platforms and models to accelerate energy efficiency finance and leverage new sources, including: Pay for Success, On-bill finance, Commercial PACE

- Finalize incentives for the Better Buildings Challenge
- Implement Pay for Success Energy Demonstration
- Convene Industry Leaders at Green Mortgage/Appraisal Roundtables

12/31/2015

Renewable Energy Target: Reach 100 MW Installed capacity by 2020 in federally subsidized housing

- Complete baseline inventory of installed capacity for 2014
- Launch partnership with DOE/NREL to provide technical support and analysis for properties in HUD's portfolio
- Reach 30 MW of installed on-site renewable energy by the end of 2015
- Highlight best practices via national and regional convenings and visibility events (Champions of Change)
- Finalize and implement policies to encourage renewable energy deployment

Date TBD

Complete development of CNA E-Tool

Date TBD

Complete energy cost and savings model for HUD-assisted properties

Date TBD

Expand health insurance reimbursement pilot for asthma to include an additional 3 localities

Date TBD

Make Healthy Homes Grant Management System operational for 95% of FY 2010 – 2013 grantees

To track our progress towards this objective, HUD will monitor the following performance indicator.

○ Agency Priority Goal Measure:

▶ ○ **Number of HUD-assisted or -associated units completing energy efficient and healthy retrofits or new construction**
To assess our progress towards increasing the energy efficiency and health of the nation's housing stock, HUD tracks the number of new or retrofitted housing units that are healthy, energy-efficient, or meet green building standards. This measure tracks the number of retrofits and units of new construction meeting energy efficiency and/or healthy home standards.

FY11 Actual	FY12 Actual	FY13 Actual	FY14 Target	FY15 Target
104,639	84,993	75,951	74,297	84,934

FY 2012-2013 & FY 2014-2015 Agency Priority Goal · Green and Healthy Homes

Between October 1, 2011 and September 30, 2013, HUD aimed to increase the energy efficiency and health of the nation's housing stock by enabling 159,000 cost-effective energy efficient or healthy housing units, as part of a joint HUD-DOE (Department of Energy) goal of 520,000 units in 2012-2013 and a total goal of 1.2 million units from 2010 through 2013. HUD exceeded its two-year goal by 1,944 units.

Learn more about this Agency Priority Goal on Performance.gov.

	Target	Actual[b]	Change from Previous Year	Target Met?
Number of HUD-assisted units completing energy efficient and healthy retrofits or new construction To assess our progress towards increasing the energy efficiency and health of the nation's housing stock, HUD tracks the number of new or retrofitted housing units that are healthy, energy-efficient, or meet green building standards. This measure tracks the number of retrofits and units of new construction meeting energy efficiency and/or healthy home standards.				
2010	55,985	88,375	NA	✓
2011	103,348	104,639	+15,264 (↑18%)	✓
2012	75,670	84,993	-19,646 (↓19%)	✓
2013	83,330[b]	75,951	-9,042 (↓10%)	✗
2012+2013 combined two-year goal	159,000[b]	160,944		✓
net change, 2010 – 2013		+353,958 energy efficient and healthy retrofits or newly constructed units		

[ᵀ] Annual performance represents progress achieved during each fiscal year, October 1ˢᵗ to September 30ᵗʰ

[ᵃ]Includes the use of a unit equivalent method approved by OMB for certain programs to reflect the ten most cost effective Energy Conservation Measures.

[ᵇ]This total includes 18,361 "stretch units." Stretch units are units needed to meet the overall two-year goal of 159,000 units, but which are not included in programmatic targets. In this case, since the program targets for FY 2012-2013 total 140,639, one must subtract 140,639 from 159,000 to arrive at 18,361 stretch units.

FY 2012-2013 & FY 2014-2015 Agency Priority Goal - Green and Healthy Homes[43]

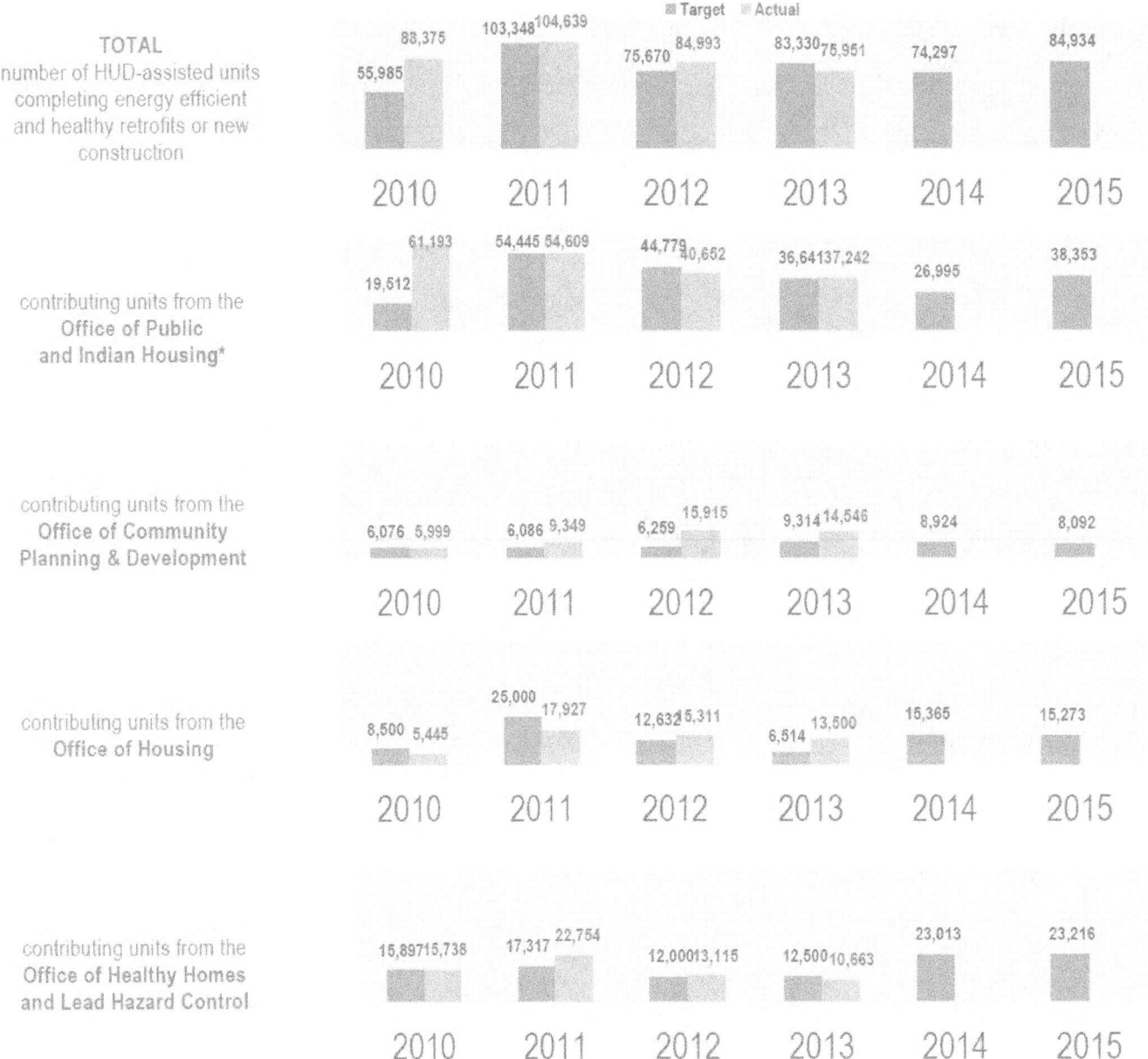

TOTAL number of HUD-assisted units completing energy efficient and healthy retrofits or new construction

Target / Actual

	2010	2011	2012	2013	2014	2015
	55,985 / 88,375	103,348 / 104,639	75,670 / 84,993	83,330 / 75,951	74,297	84,934

contributing units from the **Office of Public and Indian Housing***

2010	2011	2012	2013	2014	2015
19,512 / 61,193	54,445 / 54,609	44,779 / 40,652	36,641 / 37,242	26,995	38,353

contributing units from the **Office of Community Planning & Development**

2010	2011	2012	2013	2014	2015
6,076 / 5,999	6,086 / 9,349	6,259 / 15,915	9,314 / 14,546	8,924	8,092

contributing units from the **Office of Housing**

2010	2011	2012	2013	2014	2015
8,500 / 5,445	25,000 / 17,927	12,632 / 5,311	6,514 / 13,500	15,365	15,273

contributing units from the **Office of Healthy Homes and Lead Hazard Control**

2010	2011	2012	2013	2014	2015
15,897 / 15,738	17,317 / 22,754	12,000 / 13,115	12,500 / 10,663	23,013	23,216

---

[43] Annual performance represents progress achieved during each fiscal year, October 1st to September 30th. Totals for FY10-11 reflect reporting from the FY2012 Annual Performance Report, and may need to be updated based on most recent reporting from grantees. *The PIH historical total for 2011 includes 1,627 new units certified as green that were funded by Recovery Act funds. Since that category of units was not included in the original 2010-2011 High-Priority Performance Goals, this total will not match prior reporting on the priority goal. It is included here to reflect HUD's methodology for the 2012-2013 Agency Priority Goal.

FY 2012-2013 Agency Priority Goal — Green and Healthy Homes

PROGRESS UPDATE

Between October 1, 2011 and September 30, 2013, HUD aimed to increase the energy efficiency and health of the nation's housing stock by enabling 159,000 cost-effective energy efficient or healthy housing units, as part of a joint HUD-DOE (Department of Energy) goal of 520,000 units in 2012-2013 and a total goal of 1.2 million units from 2010 through 2013. HUD exceeded its two-year goal by 1,944 units.

HUD also exceeded its target for the four-year period since this APG was established (FY 2010-13) with more than 350,000 energy-efficient and green units completed, and a combined total with the Department of Energy of more than 1.4 million units. This significant success will occur because HUD exceeded its FY 2012 target by 12% and also exceeded its FY 2010-2011 target by 21%.

The FY2012-2013 total includes 21,265[44] units using the unit equivalent method approved by OMB, derived using the ten most cost effective Energy Conservation Measures reported through the Public Housing Capital Fund and Office of Native American Programs. Units reported include both retrofits of existing units as well as new units meeting the Energy Star for Certified Homes standard.

- Agency-wide, HUD has completed 160,944 energy or healthy green retrofits through the end of FY 2013, surpassing its cumulative goal of 159,000 units. Of these, 137,166 units, or 85 percent, were energy-related, and the remaining 23,778 units were lead hazard control and healthy homes retrofits funded through HUD's Office of Healthy Homes and Lead Hazard Control.

- The Office of Community Planning and Development has completed a total of 30,461 energy retrofits, or 96 percent (14,894 units) ahead of its cumulative target of 15,573 units. CPD units consist primarily of new Low Income Housing Tax Credit units funded through the Tax Credit Assistance Program (TCAP) as well as new HOME and CDBG-funded units meeting the Energy Star Certified Homes standard.

- The Office of Housing has completed 28,811 units, ahead of its target of 19,146 units by 50 percent (9,665 units). This number includes some single family units using FHA's PowerSaver Title I energy home improvement loans, but consists primarily of multifamily housing such as Section 202 and Section 811 housing for the elderly and disabled persons, the ARRA-funded Green Retrofit Program, and FHA multifamily endorsements with green features.

- The Office of Healthy Homes and Lead Hazard Control completed 23,778 green and healthy units, lagging slightly behind their target of 24,500 by 3 percent (722 units). OHHLHC reports on a variety of lead hazard control and healthy housing grant programs, as well as enforcement actions and the Green and Healthy Homes Initiative which combines energy efficient and health interventions. In both FY 2012 and 2013, OHHLHC's funding was reduced, resulting in fewer lead hazard control grants. Grantees also experienced increased costs per housing unit, and less additional funding from local sources (leveraging), which resulted in fewer units being completed than projected.

---

[44] This figure currently includes PHCF (non-ARRA) and ONAP units.

- The Office of Public and Indian Housing has completed 77,894 retrofits and new green units, slightly lagging behind their target of 81,420 by 4 percent (3,526 units). This slight lag was primarily because the FY 2012 target for Energy Performance Contracts was not met; however, the FY 2013 target for EPCs was exceeded. PIH units include completed Energy Performance Contracts utilizing third party financing; units using Capital Funds for energy upgrades, as reported for the first time using the Energy and Performance Information Center (EPIC) data system; as well as some completed HOPE VI Energy Star units.

Ongoing challenges include the complex regulatory requirements for updating minimum energy standards for new housing; limited tools to incentivize energy efficiency in some programs; the continuing need for a uniform baseline for residential energy consumption across the portfolio; and limitations on the Department's ability to collect consistent energy consumption data.

To continue to track HUD's quarterly and annual progress on this goal, visit Performance.gov.

Strategic Objective 4C: Disaster Resilience

Support the recovery of communities from disasters by promoting community resilience, developing state and local capacity, and ensuring a coordinated federal response that reduces risk and produces a more resilient built environment

OVERVIEW

Helping to increase communities' resilience is integral to national preparedness and the mission of HUD. This effort is consistent with the goals and objectives of Presidential Policy Directive / PPD-8 (National Preparedness) and Executive Order 13653 (Preparing the United States for the Impacts of Climate Change). Over the next five years, HUD will continue to support and expand programs and initiatives designed to increase and enhance pre-planning, research, infrastructure investment, partnerships, and cross-cutting coordination related to disaster response, recovery, and resilience. This work will involve the combined efforts of HUD's program offices and federal, state, local, and private sector partners and will incorporate HUD's civil rights, energy, environment, and diversity goals and responsibilities.

STRATEGIES

- **Build resilience strategies into HUD programs**, promoting the use of resilient housing, community development, land-use planning, and infrastructure investment patterns, and foster innovations in resilient rebuilding based on the latest data on current and future risk to ensure the most effective use of federal resources and reduce risks to all communities.

- **Increase capacity of state and local governments to plan for and implement long term recovery and rebuilding**, and encourage increased private and community investment and research in disaster recovery capabilities.

- **Facilitate the effective use of post-disaster housing resources, while ensuring full compliance with applicable fair housing and civil rights laws**, to restore and strengthen homes and provide families with safe, affordable housing options and to reduce the impacts of future disasters.

- **Promote regional coordination to ensure that community infrastructure investments are resilient, environmentally and fiscally sustainable, and delivered without delay.**

- **Improve data collection and information sharing across and by federal, State and local entities** to bolster disaster preparedness, response and recovery efforts.

- **In partnership with other federal agencies, lead and advance the National Disaster Recovery Framework** to ensure that interagency federal disaster recovery efforts are effectively coordinated, and that the recommendations in the Hurricane Sandy Rebuilding Task Force's Rebuilding Strategy are fully implemented for the Sandy recovery and, where applicable, for national programs and efforts.

Harriet Tregoning
Director
Office of Economic Resilience

MAJOR MILESTONES

9/30/2014   Develop metrics for tracking progress on disaster recovery & resilience

MEASURING OUR PROGRESS

To track our progress towards this objective, HUD will track the following performance indicator. Further metrics are under development.

▶ **Percentage of Sandy Task Force recommendations related to disaster recovery and resilience that have been implemented**

FY11 Actual	FY12 Actual	FY13 Actual	FY14 Target	FY15 Target
NA	NA	5%	65%	98%

Strategic Objective 4D: Community Development

Strengthen communities' economic health, resilience and access to opportunity

If hard-working people who play by the rules are to get ahead, they need to be able to access quality education and decent jobs, from a foundation of security in basic needs like personal safety, housing and food. Creating such environments requires collaboration among organizations with different roles and specialties at the local level, and federal agencies that are able to provide cross-sector support. Neighborhood, municipal, and regional environments that can attract investment and also support children and families are the backbone of inclusive and resilient economic growth. Building on the community's institutional, financial, human and physical capital is vital to economic growth and bolsters resiliency in times of disaster or downturn.

Local networks among the private sector, government, and community leaders can be particularly effective at creating lasting solutions. The federal role is to support and complement the private sector, civic institutions, states, and localities, not to supplant their efforts. An effective federal role is to catalyze private investment and market discipline by addressing market failures, frictions and gaps. HOME and CDBG, the two major formula grant programs that support housing, community and economic development, provide a strong foundation for these placed-based federal efforts.

HUD participates in several interagency place-based initiatives that focus existing funding more effectively and create incentives for collaboration across organizational, jurisdictional and sectoral lines. Such initiatives support communities in improving their growth potential and the quality of life and opportunities for their residents.

STRATEGIES

- Promise Zones build on the Administration's neighborhood revitalization work by accelerating the progress of high-poverty communities whose stakeholders have joined in a collaborative strategy with a shared commitment to results. These communities will create jobs, increase economic activity, reduce serious and violent crime, and improve educational opportunities to develop communities that serve as launching pads for their residents, as opposed to traps where poor conditions and isolation undermine the potential for success.

- Choice Neighborhoods grants support locally driven strategies to address struggling neighborhoods with distressed public or HUD-assisted housing through a comprehensive approach to neighborhood transformation. Local leaders, residents, and stakeholders, such as public housing authorities, cities, schools, police, business owners, nonprofits, and private developers, come together to create and implement a plan that transforms distressed HUD housing and addresses the challenges in the surrounding neighborhood. The program is designed to catalyze critical improvements in neighborhood assets, including vacant property, housing, services and schools.

- Strong Cities, Strong Communities (SC2) addresses the issue of reduced municipal capacity, which makes it more difficult for community leaders to use existing federal funds to their maximum potential in economic revitalization strategies. The capacity of cities and counties represents a crucial opportunity for federal intervention, because local governments receive direct allocations of formula grant funding and their elected leadership often exerts substantial influence on the governance of other local bodies receiving important grant allocations. Poor municipal capacity affects the quality and function of federally-funded services in multiple activities that contribute to – or harm – a community's ability to attract investment and create access to opportunity for its residents. SC2 supports local leaders in creating a solid foundation for growth.

- The Partnership for Sustainable Communities administers planning grants, technical assistance and support for implementation projects to regional organizations and municipalities to plan infrastructure and housing investments in such a way that they channel growth, reduce transportation inefficiencies, and promote environmental quality. When implemented effectively such plans make neighborhoods more prosperous, enhance economic competitiveness, and save households and businesses time and money on transportation, substantially improving the bottom line of business and the quality of life.

LEADING THIS OBJECTIVE

Valerie Piper
Deputy Assistant Secretary for Economic Development
Office of Community Planning & Development

Harriet Tregoning
Director
Office of Economic Resilience

Mark Linton
Executive Director
Strong Cities, Strong Communities

MAJOR MILESTONES

6/15/2014	**Launch Sustainable Communities Indicator Catalogue** This resource was developed in close partnership with DOT and EPA for use by communities who want to assess their resilience baseline and progress toward goals but have limited capacity.
12/1/2014	**Publish Initial Set of Best Practices for Achieving Resilient, Sustainable Communities** The Sustainable Communities Initiative has produced an enormous volume of material on best practices, both in the form of technical assistance from Capacity-Building Intermediaries and planning products and techniques from planning grantees. These resources will begin to be published online in a curated, searchable format so that every community can benefit from the lessons learned.
12/31/2014	**Pilot Metrics for Evaluating Sustainable Communities Planning Grants** Choose a set of sustainable communities metrics and pilot in Sustainable

Communities grantee communities

12/31/2016   Select 20 total urban, rural and tribal Promise Zones

MEASURING OUR PROGRESS
   HUD is developing metrics and milestones to track progress on this objective.

Achieving Operational Excellence: Management Challenges and Objectives

In order for HUD to achieve its program goals, HUD's operations must be efficient, effective, and serve customer needs. HUD plans to achieve operational excellence by improving planning, processes, accountability, and transparency, and also by developing and using customer feedback mechanisms.

In addition to the management objectives noted below, HUD is committed to contributing to achievement of performance goals that are major priorities for the federal government as a whole. Per the GPRA Modernization Act requirement to address Cross-Agency Priority (CAP) goals in the agency strategic plan, the annual performance plan, and the annual performance report, please refer to www.performance.gov for the agency's contributions to these goals and progress, where applicable.

For information on HUD's response to OIG's Report on Management and Performance Challenges and the GAO High Risk list, see HUD's 2013 Agency Financial Report.

Acquisitions Management Objective: Improve HUD's acquisitions performance through early collaborative planning and enhanced utilization of acquisition tools.

Departmental Clearance Management Objective: Reduce the time and complexity of the clearance process by establishing and enforcing clear protocols for drafting and reviewing documents placed in departmental clearance.

Equal Employment Opportunity Management Objective: Promote a diverse and inclusive work environment that is free of discrimination and harassment by educating the workforce on the overall Equal Employment Opportunity (EEO) process and their EEO responsibilities as managers and employees of HUD.

Financial Management Objective: Increase accuracy, speed, transparency, and accountability in financial management and budgeting for the agency.

Grants Management Objective: Make the grants management process more efficient and effective by automating and streamlining processes, improving timeliness, and tracking performance.

Human Capital Management Objective: Employ, develop, and foster a collaborative, high-performing workforce that is capable of continuing to deliver HUD's mission in a changing and uncertain future.

Information Management Objective: Make high-quality data available to those who need it, when they need it, where they need it, to support decision-making in furtherance of HUD's mission.

Organizational Structure Management Objective: Reduce the cost of leased space, utilities, travel and other related costs by adapting our business processes.

Management Objective: Acquisitions

Improve HUD's acquisitions performance through early collaborative planning and enhanced utilization of acquisition tools.

OVERVIEW

The Office of the Chief Procurement Officer (OCPO) is responsible for all HUD procurement and procurement-related activities. The acquisition process can be lengthy, partially due to necessary compliance with statutes, policies and procedures. OCPO sees an opportunity to streamline the acquisition process and increase customer satisfaction by mapping out the process and identifying and removing non-value added steps.

In this challenging economic environment, OCPO also seeks to maximize the value of every taxpayer dollar and ensure opportunities for small businesses. To accomplish this, OCPO is committed to using internal and external acquisition vehicles specifically established to leverage HUD's and the government's buying power, maximize opportunities for small business, and increase the successful outcomes of acquisitions.

STRATEGIES

- **Streamline the acquisition process.** OCPO will work to re-engineer HUD's Government Technical Representative program to comply with the Federal Acquisition Institute's Federal Acquisition Certification-Contracting Officer Representative (FAC-COR) model, professionalize the COR job series, and streamline pre- and post-award acquisition processes. As part of this effort, OCPO will lead a cross functional team to map detailed acquisition processes, identify and eliminate non-value added steps, assess the risks associated with their removal and increase customer satisfaction in the process. The cross-functional acquisition team will include representation from HUD Program Offices and support offices. OCPO will ensure compliance with the Federal Acquisition Regulation and the HUD Acquisition Regulations, Section 508 of the Rehabilitation Act of 1973, Office of Management and Budget and Small Business Administration policies, and Government Accountability Office findings during the analysis process.

- **Increase opportunities for small business.** Improve HUD's small business opportunities through enhanced market research and early collaborative planning. OCPO and the Office of Small and Disadvantaged Business Utilization (OSDBU) will develop acquisition tools and procedures to enhance market research fostering identification of a broader base of small businesses with core disciplines consistent with HUD's mission. These tools will be launched through a multi-educational approach to the acquisition workforce, including instruction, simulation, case studies and experiential sharing.

- **Optimize the use of acquisition strategies.** Utilize internal and external acquisition vehicles that leverage HUD's and the government's buying power in order to optimize successful contractual outcomes and reduce costs. These strategies include Lowest Priced Technically Acceptable – Best Value evaluation methods, strategic sourcing, non-monetary performance incentives, increased competition, shared savings, and the tactical use of fixed price and performance-based strategies.

Keith Surber

Acting Chief Procurement Officer

MAJOR MILESTONES

9/30/2015 **Implementation of new streamlined process, including for Contracting Officer Representatives**

OCPO will work to professionalize the Contracting Officer Representative job series and program at HUD in order to remove ambiguities created by our current practice, align HUD with the rest of the Federal Government, and allow for all stakeholders to participate in performance management of CORs.

MEASURING OUR PROGRESS

Standardized monthly reports and data from HUD's Acquisition Management System will support calculation of performance metrics to determine progress. The following performance indicators will be tracked.

▶ **Percentage of requisitions released by the target requisition release date (by Program Office)**
Improve customers' timely submission of acquisition requirements by the agreed-upon planned target requisition release date.

FY11 Actual	FY12 Actual	FY13 Actual	FY14 Target	FY15 Target
No Data	No Data	35%	47%	59%

▶ **Percentage of awards meeting target award date (by the Office of the Chief Procurement Officer)**
This indicator will track the percentage of awards that are made by the agreed-upon target award date, for actions released by the target requisition release date.

FY11 Actual	FY12 Actual	FY13 Actual	FY14 Target	FY15 Target
No Data	No Data	55%	67%	79%

▶ **Total number of days to contract award, by acquisition strategy**
This indicator will track the total number of days to award a contract, categorized by each of the main acquisition strategies used to make the award. FY10-11 values are not available.

Acquisition Strategy	FY13 Actual	FY14 Target	FY15 Target
8a Set Aside Sole Source	96		
Full and Open Competition	230		
Interagency Agreement	34	Tracking Only	Tracking Only
Modification: Option	37		
Sole Source Negotiated	53		

Task Order Competitive – HUD	97		
Task Order Competitive – GSA	156		
Task Order Non-Competitive Negotiated	59		
Task Order Non-Competitive Prepriced	34		

Management Objective: Departmental Clearance

> Reduce the time and complexity of the clearance process by establishing and enforcing clear protocols for drafting and reviewing documents placed in departmental clearance.

OVERVIEW

For some significant policy documents, submission of the document for departmental clearance is the first time that key HUD policy and support offices and HUD's Office of General Counsel (OGC) review such documents. The absence of involvement of key HUD offices can result in a lengthy clearance process if major disagreements exist. There are also less significant policy documents that only need abbreviated review which go through the full clearance process unnecessarily.

To address these challenges, HUD will establish guidelines for development of significant policy documents that include a preclearance process and protocols for clearance of these documents. HUD will also establish guidelines that will institute a significant reduction or no clearance of routine or less significant policy documents.

STRATEGIES

- **Establish guidelines for development of pre-clearance process.** Protocols will be issued to clarify that the preclearance process is for significant policy documents, such as documents that implement new law (e.g., the Violence Against Women Reauthorization, 2013, defining Qualified Mortgages for HUD, or new NOFAs) or changes to longstanding HUD policies and practices such as Affirmatively Furthering Fair Housing. With respect to the clearance process itself, the review time will be tailored dependent upon whether the clearance item presents new significant policy or legal mandates. Such items will go through full clearance, with a goal of completing review in two weeks. Clearance items not falling into this category will go through an abbreviated and limited review process.

- **Ensure transparency by utilizing a department-wide clearance calendar.** The Clearance Calendar allows everyone within HUD to see the current version of a document in clearance, all clearance comments and resolutions, and the context, major issues, and priorities for each document. By increasing use of the clearance calendar, the clearance process will be much more transparent. This will also provide an electronic record of the time it took a document to go through clearance.

LEADING THIS OBJECTIVE
Damon Smith

Office of General Counsel

MAJOR MILESTONES

9/30/2014   **Establish guidelines for development of pre-clearance process.**

        Protocols will be issued to clarify the preclearance process is for significant policy documents and clearance process review times will be tailored dependent upon new significant policy or legal mandates.

MEASURING OUR PROGRESS

To track our progress towards this objective, HUD will monitor the following key performance indicator.

► **Percentage of documents that complete the clearance process by the deadline**
HUD will monitor percentage of documents that complete the clearance process on -time. (i.e., no non-concurrences are submitted or remain unresolved).

FY11 Actual	FY12 Actual	FY13 Actual	FY14 Target	FY15 Target
NA	NA	NA	NA*	80%

*HUD's Clearance Calendar was launched in August 2013 therefore data will not be available until end 2014.

Management Objective: Equal Employment Opportunity

Promote a diverse and inclusive work environment that is free of discrimination and harassment by educating the workforce on the overall Equal Employment Opportunity (EEO) process and their EEO responsibilities as managers and employees of HUD.

OVERVIEW

The Office of Departmental Equal Employment Opportunity (ODEEO) is responsible for ensuring the enforcement of federal laws relating to the elimination of all forms of discrimination in the Department's employment practices and to ensure equal employment opportunity (EEO), promote inclusiveness, and foster a culture that values diversity and empowers the HUD workforce. Additionally, ODEEO is responsible for leading the Department's efforts to proactively prevent unlawful discrimination. ODEEO also seeks to foster an agency culture in which disputes are resolved at the lowest possible level and before a formal complaint is filed.

Currently, all managers and employees have not been trained on the overall EEO process and their EEO responsibilities. ODEEO seeks to offer training to the HUD workforce on the EEO process and the responsibilities of the workforce regarding Equal Employment Opportunity, as well as serving as a resource to the program office leadership by providing direction, guidance, and monitoring of key activities to ensure the successful implementation of the principles of EEO throughout the Department.

STRATEGIES

- **Maximize EEO training opportunities for all HUD employees.** Make quarterly training programs, workshops, and online training courses on the EEO process available to the entire HUD workforce, and provide an overview of the EEO process to new employees during their orientation sessions. Incorporate mandatory EEO training for all employees, supervisors, managers, and executives on the fundamental competencies of effective leadership through our core values.

- **Establish HUD as a model EEO program.** Integrate EEO principles into all non-supervisory employees performance standard and establish an EEO performance standard for all supervisory employees to demonstrate commitment from agency leadership. Promote the use of Alternate Dispute Resolution throughout the Department.

- **Proactively track EEO data in order to identify and address EEO issues.** Provide direction, guidance, and monitoring of key activities on a quarterly basis to ensure the successful implementation of the principles of EEO in the program areas. Conduct trend analysis to identify potential areas of concern throughout the Department and develop plans to address any identified concerns.

John Benison, *Director*

Office of Equal Employment Opportunity

MAJOR MILESTONES

None

MEASURING OUR PROGRESS

To track our progress towards this objective, HUD will monitor the following performance indicators.

▶ **Number of pre-complaint resolutions occurring through the Alternate Dispute Resolution process**
HUD will seek to increase the number of pre-complaint resolutions occurring through the Alternate Dispute Resolution process.

FY11 Actual	FY12 Actual	FY13 Actual	FY14 Target	FY15 Target
No Data	No Data	No Data	Establish Baseline	16% increase (relative to FY14 baseline)

▶ **Number of complaint filings per fiscal year**
HUD will seek to reduce the number of complaint filings per fiscal year on the basis of reprisal resulting in a hostile working environment.

FY11 Actual	FY12 Actual	FY13 Actual	FY14 Target	FY15 Target
96	67	88	79	67

Management Objective: Financial Management

Increase accuracy, speed, transparency, and accountability in financial management and budgeting for the agency.

HUD's current core accounting systems have been a source of audit findings for many years. The systems have limited functionality and are difficult to maintain properly, which increases the risk of failure. Moreover, the current budget process has limited transparency and not all staff are trained on the appropriate budget formulation procedures. Further, HUD's internal control processes need to be improved by addressing these significant deficiencies and material weaknesses.

The Office of the Chief Financial Officer (OCFO) plans to improve internal controls on financial management by reducing significant deficiencies and eliminating material weaknesses across the department. HUD will also improve the reliability of the financial accounting systems. HUD will also modify the budget formulation processes and procedures in order to increase transparency.

STRATEGIES

- **Improve internal controls.** Improve internal controls on financial management by leading cross-agency initiatives to resolve material weaknesses and significant deficiencies, and work with the Office of the Inspector General (OIG) to agree on appropriate solutions. A strategic review of financial management and budget within the department will be performed to tighten the connection between programs and OCFO to optimize its structure.

- **Improve the reliability of the financial accounting systems.** Replace the current financial accounting systems with a new shared services system to improve viability, reliability, and reporting. The new financial accounting system will:

  - Improve functionality by providing on-demand financial information and greater flexibility in creating customized reports for end-users; and
  - Provide financial information and analytical capability to complete analysis to measure the effectiveness and efficiency of program outputs and outcomes

- **Improve the budget formulation process.** OCFO will improve this process by implementing necessary system improvements and establishing an annual budget calendar with timeliness targets to circulate to program offices; create a platform to initiate and respond to customer feedback; prepare clearer budget policies and procedures with program offices; and develop and provide budget formulation training to program office staff. This will allow leadership to make more informed budgetary decisions.

David Sidari

Chief Financial Officer

MAJOR MILESTONES

9/30/2014   **Implementation of New Core Financial Management System**

Replace the current financial accounting systems with a new shared services system to improve viability, reliability, and reporting

- 9/30/2014 – Go live with updated FedTraveler module
- 2/8/2015 – Go live with updated WebTA module

9/30/2015   **Resolve HUD's material weakness and significant deficiencies.**

Resolve pertinent material weaknesses to restore OIG's audit of HUD's financial statements to an unqualified audit opinion for FY14. Additionally, establish regular communication with the OIG regarding new audit issues and a path toward resolution of existing material weaknesses and significant deficiencies toward the goal of an unqualified audit opinion in subsequent years

MEASURING OUR PROGRESS

To track our progress towards this objective, HUD will monitor completion of the milestones above.

Management Objective: Grants Management

Make the grants management process more efficient and effective by automating and streamlining processes, improving timeliness, and tracking performance.

OVERVIEW

HUD's management and oversight of grants can be more effective and efficient at a number of points over the grant life-cycle. This is the result of a number of conditions: decentralized responsibilities and unclear authorities, a lack of policy and process standardization across program offices, the existence of a multitude of grant-related IT systems for identical or similar tasks, the lack of a centralized performance reporting system, and minimal, centralized oversight of program operations.

To address these challenges, HUD will: develop a centralized, one-stop performance reporting capability for agency grants; standardize and strengthen oversight of grant-related policies and processes; improve programmatic oversight of grant programs for compliance and performance; and align and optimize grant-related IT systems agency wide.

STRATEGIES

- **Streamline the grants management process.** Strengthen and align enterprise-wide grants management responsibilities, policies, processes, and IT systems.

- **Reduce the amount of time it takes to get funds to grantees.** Assure the alignment of HUD's policies and processes and the optimization of IT systems results in decreasing the time it takes to get funds to grantees.

- **Develop comprehensive, standardized, and centralized performance reporting capability.** Evaluate, align, improve, and consolidate grantee performance information to improve HUDs visibility to inform agency decision-making and improve outcomes.

LEADING THIS OBJECTIVE

Anne Morillon
Director, Division of Grants Management and Oversight
Office of Strategic Planning and Management

Cliff Taffet
General Deputy Assistant Secretary
Office of Community Planning and Development

11/1/2014	**Complete analysis for optimization of grant related IT systems**
	Make associated recommendations for system consolidation and/or migration based on analysis.
12/31/2014	**Realign and consolidate performance data elements for an Enterprise Performance Reporting System for grants**
	Develop standardization for grantee data collection and for receiving performance data from grantees

MEASURING OUR PROGRESS

To track our progress towards this objective, HUD will monitor completion of the milestones above.

Retrospective: FY 2012-2013 Agency Priority Goal ▪ Award Funds Fairly and Quickly

Between October 1, 2011 and September 30, 2013, HUD aimed to improve internal processes to ensure that it could obligate 90 percent of Notice of Funding Availability (NOFA) programs within 180 calendar days from budget passage, ensuring that America's neediest families have the shelter and services they need, when they need them.

	Target	Actual	Change from Previous Year	Target Met?
○ **Percent of NOFA programs obligated within 180 days of budget passage**				
This indicator identifies the number of competitive grant programs or "NOFA" programs that had obligated funds within 180 days following budget passage.				
2011	NA	56%	NA	
2012	90%	46%	(↓10%)	✗
2013	90%	32%†	(↓14%)	✓

†There were 25 NOFAs in FY 2013, with 8 (32%) NOFAs making the 180 day goal (September 22, 2013).

FY 2012-2013 Agency Priority Goal ▪ Award Funds Fairly and Quickly

FINAL PROGRESS UPDATE

Through September 22, 2013, or 180 days following budget passage, the Department had obligated funds for 8 of the 25 (32%) competitive grant programs or "NOFA" programs. Within 8 days of September 22 (September 30 or the end of the fiscal year 2013), the Department had obligated funds for an additional 4 NOFA programs, bringing the rate to 48% or 12 of 25 NOFA programs. By December 31, 2013, the Department had obligated funds for two-thirds (17 of 25 or 68%) of the FY 2013 NOFA programs.

While the target for the FY12-13 performance period was not reached, HUD remains committed to awarding funds more efficiently, and several recent significant business process transformations are expected to improve and streamline the NOFA process in FY14 and beyond. Importantly, the Department is automating the NOFA processes, from NOFA development through the obligation document. The Department also contracted with a vendor to build a communications portal for its NOFA stakeholders to easily access current policies and procedures as well as provide a portal to share best practices. In September 2013, HUD entered into an agreement with the Department of Health and Human Services (HHS) Center of Excellence for Grants Management to obtain the use of software application modules to automate and streamline the grants.

It is worthwhile to note that the Department also significantly edited and enhanced the clarity of requirements outlined in the General Section for all NOFAs. The improvements to the General Section are expected to reduce the number of questions from potential grantees concerning the application requirements and facilitate NOFA development internally.

Management Objective: Human Capital

Employ, develop, and foster a collaborative, high-performing workforce that is capable of continuing to deliver HUD's mission in a changing and uncertain future.

OVERVIEW

We will employ, develop, and foster a collaborative, values-driven, and capable workforce by focusing our efforts on: 1) promoting greater leadership effectiveness, 2) enhancing employee engagement, and 3) addressing performance results.

The Department will face a number of challenges and changes in the years ahead, as we continue to address the housing recovery during a period of fiscal constraints. Changes in housing markets and communities around the nation are speeding up, just as natural disasters and the need for rebuilding communities across America is also increasing. Meanwhile, it is estimated that 57% of HUD's workforce will be eligible to retire by 2015. To accomplish our mission in the years ahead, we must capture the wisdom and knowledge of our current and departing technical experts and leaders and transmit it to their successors. In that regard, we must value and utilize more effectively the contributions of all our employees as vital members of our workforce and help them fulfill their professional development and career needs.

By improving leadership effectiveness, investing in employee engagement, and addressing performance challenges, we will build a more collaborative workforce, demonstrate our core values, and grow our capabilities. By fulfilling our roles as a trusted strategic partner, a human capital compliance expert, and a transactions facilitator for HUD's employees, we can ensure that HUD's workforce is ready to achieve its mission of creating sustainable, inclusive communities and quality, affordable homes for all.

STRATEGIES

- **Strengthening talent management.** HUD is vulnerable to losing a wealth of institutional knowledge, based on the anticipated rate of retirements and attrition in key positions over the next few years. HUD faces challenges integrating a new generation of employees into the workforce, while maximizing the talents of our existing workforce. To address these challenges, the Office of the Chief Human Capital Officer (OCHCO) will partner with our customers to deliver consultative and comprehensive talent management programs and services that put the right people in the right place doing the right things to achieve HUD's mission. We will continue to develop and deploy programs that focus on; improving the performance, development, and fit of our leadership; fully engaging our employees; and addressing performance results.

- **Achieving performance results.** OCHCO will continue promoting our core values and performance feedback at every level of the Department and equip HUD's executives, managers and employees with the tools they need to improve leader effectiveness, engage employees, identify and address performance deficiencies, and build upon existing strengths in their programs.

LEADING THIS OBJECTIVE
Mike Anderson
Chief Human Capital Officer

MAJOR MILESTONES

6/30/2014	Develop succession planning tool for assessing high impact positions and successor candidate readiness to assume these positions for succession planning purposes
12/30/2014	Identify high impact positions within all HUD offices, and develop HUD office projections of critical position vacancy risk as it relates to an office's strategic objectives
2/28/2015	Publish a departmental succession plan aligned with HUD's strategic plan

MEASURING OUR PROGRESS

To track our progress towards this objective, HUD will monitor the following key indicators:

▶ **Talent Management: HUD's score on the Employee Viewpoint Survey Engagement Index**
In order to measure the impact of activities to improve employee engagement and capability, HUD will track progress on the EVS Engagement Index.

FY11 Actual	FY12 Actual	FY13 Actual	FY14 Target	FY15 Target
61	62	57	59	62

▶ **Talent Management: Percentage of successor candidates ready to assume high impact positions**
In order to improve leadership effectiveness, HUD will implement a robust succession plan. To ensure the quality of that plan and the associated development initiatives, HUD will track the number of successor candidates ready to assume high impact positions and roles of strategic significance to the Department.

FY11 Actual	FY12 Actual	FY13 Actual	FY14 Target	FY15 Target
No Data	No Data	No Data	Establish Baseline	Target TBD

▶ **Human capital customer satisfaction scores**
In order to measure and improve our own performance in serving HUD's program offices OCHCO will track internal customer satisfaction.

FY11 Actual	FY12 Actual	FY13 Actual	FY14 Target	FY15 Target
No Data	No Data	No Data	Establish Baseline	Target TBD

Management Objective: Information Management

Make high-quality data available to those who need it, when they need it, where they need it, to support decision-making in furtherance of HUD's mission.

OVERVIEW

HUD data can be unreliable, inaccessible, and redundant, with new systems or datasets created to address faulty data rather than fixing the original data source. Moreover, HUD has historically had a fragmented approach to technology adoption, which leads to multiple platforms and multiple services competing for resources. Finally and similarly, HUD has not achieved the right balance of contracting support and in-house expertise to manage the agency's data and systems effectively and affordably.

Over the next four years, HUD aims to leverage these opportunities by enhancing the quality, availability, and delivery of HUD information to citizens, employees, business partners, and the government, while striving for excellence in IT management practices and governance to consolidate and streamline HUD's systems. In pairing enhanced technology and improved processes with a developing and strengthening workforce, the department expects to vastly broaden its ability to achieve current and future departmental goals.

STRATEGIES

- **Manage and develop HUD's IT workforce.** HUD will develop an IT human capital plan to guide the recruitment, retention, and skill development of staff. We will identify the skills desired within our IT workforce and measure current gaps, then create development programs targeting those competencies.

- **Deploy new technologies, supported by a robust data governance structure.** We will use new technologies to more quickly and reliably gather and disseminate data, and provide better IT services to our staff and clients, including full compliance with Section 508 of the Rehabilitation Act of 1973 and the additional provision of reasonable accommodations as necessary. We will develop a data governance structure and data protocols that will ensure our data are accurate and authoritative, and remove processes or data that are redundant or unnecessary.

- **Consolidate IT infrastructure.** HUD will reduce the number of systems in order to reduce operating costs, achieve interoperability, increase collaboration among operating divisions, improve customer service, and provide a secure and trusted IT environment ensuring confidentiality, integrity, and availability of IT resources.

LEADING THIS OBJECTIVE

Kevin Cooke

Acting Chief Information Officer

| 6/30/2015 | **Develop and implement an IT Human Capital Plan** |
| | Develop comprehensive plan to guide the recruitment, training, and retention of IT specialists, along with a long-term approach to strategically supplement in-house expertise with skilled contracting services. |

| 6/30/2015 | **Establish a consolidated IT infrastructure** |
| | Identify obsolete applications and create decommissioning schedule in order to streamline HUD systems. Refine IT governance processes to ensure collaborative approach to It infrastructure investment and maintenance |

| 6/30/2015 | **Develop and implement a data governance structure** |
| | Through data governance working group, develop strong data governance structure. Identify single, authoritative source for all HUD data collected, as well as a data owner for each set of data and work to consolidate data into a single location with common data elements across multiple data sets. |

MEASURING OUR PROGRESS

To track our progress towards this objective, HUD will monitor the following key performance indicators:

▶ **Number of IT systems**
Total number of HUD IT systems

FY11 Actual	FY12 Actual	FY13 Actual	FY14 Target	FY15 Target
No Data	No Data	216	205	195

▶ **Cost of IT systems (in millions)**
Total cost of operating and maintaining HUD IT systems, excluding infrastructure

FY11 Actual	FY12 Actual	FY13 Actual	FY14 Target	FY15 Target
$88,062,343	$97,948,771	$107,084,731	$101,730,494 (5% reduction)	5% reduction from FY14

▶ **IT customer service satisfaction scores**
Conduct an annual survey of HUD staff on satisfaction with IT services provided.

FY11 Actual	FY12 Actual	FY13 Actual	FY14 Target	FY15 Target
No Data	No Data	No Data	Establish Baseline	Target TBD

Management Objective: Organizational Structure

Reduce the cost of leased space, utilities, travel and other related costs by adapting our business processes.

OVERVIEW

Even despite recent advances in programs such as telework and alternative work schedules, HUD has historically operated with a traditional definition of the workplace. This objective intends to help HUD redefine the workplace as more than just an office, but rather the combination of people and information brought together by technology which allows work to be done at any appropriate location.

In order to measure our success in this endeavor, HUD intends to reduce the amount of space per employee and contractor. Ultimately, this will reduce the total dollars that we spend on leased space, building maintenance, utilities, travel, and other related costs. In order to achieve these efficiencies, HUD will work with the General Services Administration to identify opportunities to reduce space through better use of technology and expanded use of external resources and partnerships.

Additionally, HUD could better meet our customers' needs by more appropriately distributing our workload and personnel by organizational unit. HUD will assess its current staff allocation, workload distribution and community needs in order to align resources to better serve our customers. In this effort, our goal is not to save money at the expense of our customers, but rather to replace outdated business practices with new business models, ultimately producing greater efficiencies, saving money, establishing sustainable business models, and most importantly better serving our customers.

STRATEGIES

- **Identify opportunities to reduce space through better use of technology** GSA will lead an initiative to understand our work processes, ultimately resulting in a set of options to utilize technology and change our work processes to reduce space.

- **Get our work in the right organizational unit** With the ultimate goal of producing greater efficiencies and better serving our customers, HUD will take advantage of new business models, e.g. consolidating offices and leveraging external resources and partnerships.

LEADING THIS OBJECTIVE

Michael Anderson

Chief Human Capital Officer

Officer of the Chief Human Capital Officer

MAJOR MILESTONES

9/30/2014	Identify opportunities to reduce space through better use of technology. GSA will lead an initiative at no cost to HUD to develop a set of options to reduce space.
9/30/2014	HUD's Office of Multifamily Housing will consolidate 10 offices from around the country.

MEASURING OUR PROGRESS

To track our progress towards this objective, HUD will monitor the following performance indicators:

- **Amount of money spent on space and travel (in millions)**

   Total dollars spent on leased space, building maintenance, utilities, travel and other related costs.

FY11 Actual	FY12 Actual	FY13 Actual	FY14 Target	FY15 Target
$267	$265	$277	Establish Baseline*	Target TBD*

   Targets to be developed based on outcome of GSA effort.

- **Space Utilization (in sq. ft.)**

   Average square footage of usable workspace per employee and contractor.

FY11 Actual	FY12 Actual	FY13 Actual	FY14 Target	FY15 Target
316	329	352	342	335

Section 3: Additional Information

Evaluating Our Strategies and Measuring Our Progress

The Government Performance and Results Act (GPRA) Modernization Act of 2010 calls upon agencies to use evaluation and research evidence to identify evidence-based strategies for reaching intended objectives. HUD continuously conducts research and evaluation to develop HUD's strategies for achieving its strategic goals and to inform budgetary allocations based on information about the cost-effectiveness of HUD's efforts. Ongoing and planned evaluations that are particularly informative for each of HUD's strategic goals are summarized below. The initiation and scope of these evaluations depends on sufficient funding. A number of these research efforts are proposed for funding in **HUD's FY 2015 budget request for the Transformation Initiative Fund**, and subsequent budget requests will identify new priorities. Additionally, readers may consult the continually updated research and evaluation resources available at **huduser.org**.

Additionally, HUD conducts regular data-driven performance reviews—"HUDStat" meetings—which focus on quarterly progress towards achieving each of HUD's priority goals. The Secretary and senior leadership from throughout the agency, and sometimes from partner agencies, attend these meetings to address challenges, review metrics, improve internal and external collaboration, and increase performance. For each objective, the Department will link specific contributing programs through its participation in the **Federal Program Inventory**. Progress on achieving each of the strategic objectives will be assessed during data-driven review meetings, published in HUD's Annual Performance Report each year, and shared on **Performance.gov**.

THE RESEARCH ROADMAP

HUD's *Research Roadmap FY 2014—FY 2018* identifies critical policy questions and will guide HUD's research investments over the next four years. The Research Roadmap, published in July of 2013, is available at **http://www.huduser.org/portal/pdf/Research_Roadmap.pdf**. Formulated by HUD's Office of Policy Development and Research (PD&R), the Roadmap has been a highly collaborative, forward looking effort to identify critical policy questions that should guide PD&R research investments over the next five years. The Roadmap team met with members of Congress, officials from the Office of Management and Budget, the Government Accountability Office, federal sister agencies, and numerous research, practitioner, and advocacy organizations to gather relevant feedback, and over 950 comments were received from stakeholders during development.

To complement the Roadmap's structured evaluation agenda, HUD seeks to expand successful use of competitive research grants and non-competitive research partnerships to better utilize external expertise in evaluating local innovations and program effectiveness. HUD's Research Partnership program is already supporting a number of high value research projects that align with HUD's mission but were proposed by outside researchers and are supported by a 50 percent match of funds from an external source.

Research and Evaluations Informing Goal 1: Strengthen the Nation's Housing Market To Bolster the Economy and Protect Consumers

<u>Currently Funded</u>

Pre-Purchase Homeownership Counseling Demonstration. HUD is working with three national lenders to conduct a random-assignment experiment to test the impacts of pre-purchase housing counseling for first-time homebuyers. HUD seeks supplemental funding for the 42-month follow-up survey (36 months after random assignment plus 6 months after counseling completion) and long-term impact analysis. An interim report on baseline characteristics is expected in 2016.

<u>Not Currently Funded</u>

Assessing the Effectiveness of Mortgage Modification Protocols. Three interrelated studies will evaluate the success of alternative policies used to preserve homeownership and support the national recovery from the foreclosure crisis, including an examination of the Department of Treasury's Home Affordable Modification Program (HAMP), FHA-HAMP, USDA-HAMP, the principal reduction alternative, the second lien modification, and proprietary protocols followed by servicers.

Impact of Real Estate Owned Properties on Neighborhoods. This project will integrate emerging research and collect outcome data about REO portfolios and their impacts, with special focus on the FHA portfolio. Results will be integrated into the Neighborhood Stabilization Program evaluation framework for tracking both past and future impacts.

Impact of the Foreclosure Crisis on HUD Programs and the Rental Market. This analysis of administrative and market data before and after the housing market crash will systematically map the long-term implications for HUD's affordable rental housing programs. A forecasting and scenario planning component will enhance HUD's capacity to anticipate and mitigate the impact of future booms and busts on its programs.

Non-retention Alternatives to Foreclosure. This research will survey the practice of short sales of homes with delinquent loans and assess the net costs and benefits for borrowers, lenders, insurers, and neighborhoods.

Impact of Qualified Mortgage Rules. This study will assess the impact of Qualified Mortgage (QM) rules on FHA, the government sponsored enterprises, the housing finance market, and borrowers.

Reverse Mortgage Study. Substantial changes in the reverse mortgage sector, combined with house price declines, have resulted in increased Home Equity Conversion Mortgage (HECM) losses to FHA. Interrelated components of this effort include an evaluation of FHA's HECM program, a new integrated dataset, a survey and analysis of local property taxes and hazard insurance rates that affect HECM defaults, and a study of incentives for HECM loan originators.

What Do We Know About Vacancy? Review of Housing Inventory and Vacancy Statistics. This project will review literature and data methods to determine how vacancy data, both public and private, are obtained, reported, and interpreted. It also will analyze how existing data on the housing stock, and vacant units in particular, could have improved understanding of the housing bubble.

Demonstration of Section 203(k) Rehabilitation Financing for Investors. This demonstration will test whether program enhancements and safeguards for FHA's Section 203(k) mortgage insurance program can make more financing available for rehabilitation, or purchase and rehabilitation, of single-family rental properties (1-4 units).

Small Multifamily Mortgage Insurance Demonstration. HUD seeks to evaluate the FY 2014 initiative to use FHA's Risk Sharing Program to facilitate the financing of small multifamily properties (5–49 units) by housing finance agencies, community development financial institutions, and other mission-driven lenders.

Research and Evaluations Informing Goal 2: Meet the Need for Quality Affordable Rental Homes
Currently Funded

Assessment of Native American, Alaska Native and Native Hawaiian Housing Needs. At the request of Congress, HUD is assessing housing quality and affordability for Native Americans, Alaska Natives, and Native Hawaiians and evaluating how the Native American Housing Assistance and Self-Determination Act (NAHASDA) has addressed those needs. An interim report is available and a report on housing needs based on in-depth surveys of properties in Indian Country and interviews with housing providers is expected to be available in 2015.

Housing Choice Voucher Program Administrative Fee Study. HUD is currently evaluating how much it costs for a Public Housing Agency to run an efficient HCV program, with the objective of supporting development of a funding formula for allocating administrative fees.

Rent Reform Demonstration. In 2012, HUD initiated a randomized controlled trial to rigorously test alternatives to the current HUD assisted rent structure among PHAs designated as Moving To Work agencies. HUD will report on the impact of the demonstration on earnings, employment, hardship, and administrative cost.

Evaluation of Jobs Plus: Baseline Phase. This evaluation will include data collection, analysis and a baseline survey at the public housing sites that are selected for participation in the first year of the Jobs Plus Initiative grant awards. The goal will be to provide evidence-based findings, lessons learned and identify operational obstacles that a larger scale implementation of the Initiative would need to address.

Moving to Work Demonstration: Baseline Phase. Congress has funded one or more studies of the extent to which the demonstration meets its statutory goals of enhancing self-sufficiency, expanding choice, and reducing administrative cost.

PBRA Transfer Authority Evaluation. At various times Congress has authorized the transfer of project-based rental assistance (PBRA) subsidies from one assisted multifamily property to another. The proposed evaluation would include a study of the impact on the cost-effectiveness of the subsidies provided and any improvements in the physical and financial condition of the subsidized housing stock.

Rental Assistance Demonstration Evaluation. This evaluation will examine the Rental Assistance Demonstration's (RAD) success in the goal to convert public housing and other HUD-assisted properties to long-term project-based Section 8 rental assistance. Impact on families and on the physical and financial viability of the projects will be evaluated through a comparison group of projects that don't go through the conversion process.

Small Area Fair Market Rent (SAFMR) Demonstration. Preliminary evidence from the 2011 implementation of SAFMRs in the Dallas, TX metropolitan area reveals slight increases in unit quality and neighborhood quality for tenants at no additional cost to the government. This demonstration is investigating the ramifications for the HCV program of implementing SAFMRs on a national scale.

Worst Case Housing Needs. PD&R uses in-house staff resources and the American Housing Survey to report to Congress biennially on the causes and trends of worst case needs for affordable rental housing.[45] Worst case needs data are widely used in the Department's budget, policy and strategic planning decisions. The next report using the forthcoming 2013 AHS data is expected in early 2015.

<u>Not Currently Funded</u>

Assessing Housing Quality in the Housing Choice Voucher Program: Design Phase. This project will fund design and testing of an updated and revised survey instrument for a survey of a representative sample of Section 8 vouchers at all public housing agencies. The results of a fully implemented survey can be used by PHAs directly to improve their communication, oversight, training and enforcement of their inspectors and by HUD to identify program improvements and to target technical assistance and oversight resources in a cost-effective manner.

Assessment of Landlord Behavior in the Housing Choice Voucher Program. This study will explore how landlord behavior affects the effectiveness of the HCV program across a range of measures including voucher success rates and tenant mobility. The study will help inform decisions on possible streamlining and improvement of the Section 8 program.

Comparing Subsidy Costs of Federal Housing Assistance Programs. This project, which will be conducted only in-house during fiscal year 2014, will examine the cost-effectiveness of existing federal housing programs as they operate across different regions and metropolitan areas of the country, and across cities, suburbs and rural areas.

Examining Small PHA Performance. This study will survey a sample of small PHAs to assess their performance levels and reasons for their performance, administrative costs, and challenges. This research is particularly relevant and timely because of the new proposed Small Housing Authority Reform Proposal (SHARP) legislation.

Improving HUD Measures of Housing Cost Inflation. This study will take advantage of improved data and recent program evaluations to analyze the comparative costs of providing a unit of housing with various housing subsidy programs. The evaluation also will examine the role of subsidy layering, the characteristics of cost-effective housing subsidy programs, and the benefits of various program approaches.

Leased Housing Tenant Payment Insurance Demonstration. HUD is seeking to design a demonstration of a new, shallow subsidy leased housing insurance program that would cover a portion of a low-income household's rent in the event of acute income shocks resulting from unemployment or health problems. Such a shallow subsidy would complement existing deep rental assistance programs by providing a safety net to support tenants who move into market-rate housing.

Utility Cost Data System. This project will collect representative tenant utility expenditures and compare them with the allowances the same tenants actually received, and those they would have received if the PHA or project owner had used the HUD Utility Schedule Model (HUSM).

---

[45] The most recent report is available at
http://www.huduser.org/portal/publications/affhsg/wc_HsgNeeds11_report.html.

Research and Evaluations Informing Goal 3: Use Housing as a Platform for Improving Quality of Life

Currently Funded

Characteristics of HUD-Assisted Households. This project will expand and leverage the capabilities of matched data sources to provide detailed information about characteristics of typical HUD-assisted renter households, such as employment, work search, health, educational pursuits, seeking permanent residences, and decisions to move.

Impact of Housing and Services Interventions on Homeless Families (Family Options Study). This random-assignment trial was initiated at the request of Congress to assess the effectiveness of four interventions for helping homeless families with children: 1) project-based transitional housing, 2) community-based rapid re-housing; 3) housing choice voucher/public housing; or 4) usual care. An interim report about initial lease-up is available, and a report on 18 month outcomes is due early in 2015.

Family Self-Sufficiency (FSS) Demonstration. This random-assignment demonstration at a large number of PHAs will measure the extent to which the FSS program contributes to increases in tenant incomes and wealth.

Choice Neighborhoods Demonstration. HUD is assessing what happens to residents, assisted developments, and surrounding neighborhoods as result of the Choice Neighborhoods Demonstration. An interim report documenting baseline conditions at the five implementation sites is available, and a second interim report about the implementation of revitalization strategies in the funded neighborhoods is due in 2014.

Evaluation of Support and Services at Home (SASH). HUD is supporting this study through an inter-agency agreement with the Department of Health and Human Services. The research will link HUD administrative data with Medicare and Medicaid claims data to evaluate the impact of affordable housing with services on the well-being and health care utilization of low-income seniors.

Evaluation of the Section 202 Supportive Housing Program for Elderly Households. This experimental design evaluation will assess the extent to which supportive housing allows elderly persons to live independently and age in place, improves their general wellbeing and health, and creates costs savings in the healthcare system.

Evaluation of the Section 811 Project Rental Assistance Demonstration. As mandated by the Melville Act, this evaluation will analyze the implementation and results of the Section 811 Project Rental Assistance Demonstration, which focuses on integrating persons with disabilities into multifamily developments, and analyze its effectiveness compared to traditional Section 811 program and to alternative housing and institutional care options for people with disabilities.

Seniors and Services Demonstration: Launch Phase. This demonstration will build on the research design and evaluation work currently underway to launch a demonstration and evaluation of seniors aging in place with services.

Understanding Rapid Re-housing: Models and Outcomes for Homeless Households. This study will seek to identify the most common program models being implemented under the rubric of a rapid re-housing intervention, and track the outcomes of households served through the various program models.

Effect of Housing Assistance Over Time. This project will review and summarize existing evidence about the effect of housing assistance over time. It will attempt to estimate the cost structure and cost effectiveness of different HUD programs using results from these analyses.

Homelessness Prevention Demonstration. This project would make a timely investment to extend the knowledge gained from HUD's recent investments in homelessness research and local innovation.

State Olmstead Plans and Assessment of Demand, Available Resources and Needs. This project will help the Department better align its programs and resources to meet the affordable housing needs for people with disabilities in integrated settings as required under the Supreme Court's Olmstead decision. It will include an estimate of housing needs for people with disabilities and a review of state enforcement and implementation of Olmstead.

Successful Exits from Targeted Housing Assistance Programs for Vulnerable Population. This study would develop a series of case studies that explore successful local strategies to enable people residing in supportive housing or other housing designed for vulnerable populations to move on into "mainstream" housing. Such policies and programs that support "moving up" or graduation to mainstream housing programs help ensure that permanent supportive housing is available for the households most in need of such intensive assistance.

Evaluation of Supportive Housing for Prisoner Reentry. This evaluation will help build an evidence-based approach for improving reentry outcomes for formerly incarcerated individuals and their communities through permanent supportive housing linked with employment, behavioral health services, and family unification. HUD is considering options ranging from an evaluation of existing PHA reentry programs to an interagency effort that would involve leveraging private/philanthropic investments to support permanent supportive housing plus services within a pay-for-success framework.

Research and Evaluations Informing Strategic Goal 4: Build Strong, Resilient, and Inclusive Communities

Currently Funded

Housing Discrimination Studies (HDS). Over several decades, rigorous testing methods have proven to be the most reliable way to assess and measure the extent and limitations of compliance with the Fair Housing Act. Several ongoing or planned Housing Discrimination Studies focus on discrimination against groups that pose methodological challenges for established testing methods, including groups that are not covered by the Fair Housing Act, but may be covered under state and local fair housing laws.

- **HDS – Families with Children.** This pilot study will test methods to measure the forms and prevalence of discrimination against families with children in rental housing, taking into account potentially interacting factors, such as age, gender, number of children and race and ethnicity.

- **HDS – Source of Income.** This study will develop methods for measuring discrimination against voucher holders in U.S. rental housing markets.

- **HDS – Lesbian, Gay, Bisexual, and Transgender People.** This study pilots techniques to obtain a baseline in-person measure of housing discrimination faced by same-sex couples in at least two metropolitan rental markets. The study will also include a pilot test of discrimination against transgender people in a single metropolitan market.

- **HDS – on the Basis of Mental Disabilities.** The study will test methods to measure the degree to which people with mental disabilities experience discrimination in the search for rental housing, conduct pilot testing, analyze HUD's discrimination complaints and compliance tracking system, and produce papers to expand the field's understanding of housing discrimination against persons with mental disabilities.

- **HDS – Persons Who Are Deaf or Who Use a Wheelchair.** This study will obtain statistically valid national estimates of the incidence of housing discrimination in the rental market against two categories of people with disabilities: persons who are deaf and hard of hearing, and persons with physical disabilities who use a wheelchair.

- **Housing Search for Racial and Ethnic Minorities.** This study is examining the processes by which racial and ethnic minorities search for rental housing.

Not Currently Funded

Affirmatively Furthering Fair Housing Study. Contingent upon the publication of a Final Rule, this evaluation of HUD's Affirmatively Furthering Fair Housing (AFFH) policy will examine the implementation of the new AFFH rule, the extent and quality of compliance, and the extent to which it is working to reduce segregation and increase affordable-housing supply. This research addresses questions posed by Research Roadmap stakeholders.

Interaction of Anchor Institutions with Neighborhoods. This study would examine the incentives leading anchor institutions use to engage with their communities, the impact of anchor institutions (especially universities and hospitals) on neighborhood income mixing, transformation and stabilization, and variation of neighborhood outcomes with respect to type of neighborhood interaction. This research addresses questions posed by Research Roadmap stakeholders.

Accelerating Post-Disaster Community Recovery. In response to Hurricane Sandy, a number of new approaches toward long-term recovery are being tested, including more regional and holistic federal coordination, an emphasis on better planning, and increased access and use of federal data for local program operations. This research will document those efforts and inform development of mechanisms that enable local governments to launch long-term recovery programs more quickly.

CDBG-Funded Disaster Recovery: Retrospective Evaluation. In recent years, Congress has increasingly relied on special appropriations to HUD's Community Development Block Grant program to provide flexible disaster recovery funds to stricken communities. This retrospective evaluation will review the characteristics and extent of disasters over the past decade, the federal response to those disasters using the CDBG-Disaster vehicle, the program's implementation, and the uses and effectiveness of those resources relative to needs.

Data Sources, Limitations and Advantages, and Validation

This section is organized by strategic goal, measure and program.

Strategic Goal 1	Strengthen the Nation's Housing Market to Bolster the Economy and Protect Consumers
Strategic Objective 1A	Establish a sustainable housing finance system that provides support during market disruptions, with a properly defined role for the U.S. government.
Metric	*Overall market share of private capital, GSEs, and FHA* • **Description:** This measure will track the share of the mortgage market for private lenders, government-sponsored entities (Fannie Mae and Freddie Mac), and FHA in order to observe FHA's role in the housing market and the balance of the housing market • **Data source:** FHA Single Family Data Warehouse, Corelogic TrueStandings; Mortgage Bankers Association of America • **Unit of measurement:** Share of market • **Dimension:** Percent • **Calculation method:** Share of specified mortgage market over share of entire market • **Frequency:** (of reporting): Quarterly • **Direction:** Downwards • **Data quality (limitations/advantages of the data):** We are relying upon CoreLogic TrueStandings loan servicing data for shares by funding source, and MBa for total market origination volumes. CoreLogic coverage of the market has slipped in recent years because subscribing lenders have been selling major servicing portfolios to non-subscribing lenders. CoreLogic is actively recruiting these new non-bank lenders and re-populating its database for 2012 and 2013. The MBa volumes are estimates and subject to error as shares of originations coming through different funding channels changes in real time from what is assumed in the MBa algorithms. Over the last two years, this has led to large revisions in market-size estimates with the release of the annual HMDA LAR data (in September). • **Measurement Validation, verification, and improvement of measure:** Inside Mortgage Finance publishes its own estimates of agency versus nonagency lending, and we can use that as a reasonability check on our estimates. • **Sequence:** 1
Strategic Objective 1B	Ensure equal access to sustainable housing financing and achieve a more balanced housing market, particularly in underserved communities.
Metric	*Federal Housing Administration share of originations* • **Description:** This measure will show the percentage of mortgage originations in the housing market that were made by FHA. • **Data source:** FHA Single Family Data Warehouse, Corelogic TrueStandings; Mortgage Bankers Association of America • **Unit of measurement:** Percent of FHA Mortgage Originations • **Dimension:** Percent • **Calculation method:** Share of specified mortgage market over share of entire market • **Frequency:** (of reporting): Quarterly • **Direction:** Downwards • **Data quality (limitations/advantages of the data):** We rely upon the MBa for total volumes and CoreLogic for average loan amounts (used to derive loan counts). See limitations on these sources in SO 1A. • **Measurement Validation, verification, and improvement of measure:** We discuss data quality with MBa and with CoreLogic, and have open communications to express any concerns.

	• **Sequence**: 2
Metric	*Percentage of loans endorsed with credit score < 680*
	• **Description:** This measure will track the percentage of FHA loans endorsed that have borrowers with a credit score under 680.
	• **Data source:** FHA Single Family Data Warehouse (FHA Single-Family Origination Trends Report)
	• **Unit of measurement:** Loans endorsed that have borrowers with a credit score less than 680
	• **Dimension:** Percent
	• **Calculation method:** Number of FHA loans endorsed with a credit score less than 680 divided by the total number of FHA loans with a credit score (those with no score excluded)
	• **Frequency:** Quarterly
	• **Direction:** Increased
	• **Data quality (limitations/advantages of the data):** Quality is good; Credit score data comes to HUD via the TOTAL Scorecard, which leverages various private AUS platforms which pull credit scores directly from the credit repositories.
	• **Measurement Validation, verification, and improvement of measure**: "Equal access" should not be defined solely by borrower credit score. Lower credit scores mean higher risk of not being able to manage the financial responsibility of large fixed debt payments and other requirements of homeownership. The goal could rather be defined by income level or minority concentrations in geographic areas.
	• **Sequence**: 3
Metric	*Percentage of loans endorsed with credit score <680 that evidence successful homeownership over the first five years*
	• **Description:** This measure will track the percentage of loans endorsed with credit score less than 680 that evidence successful homeownership over the first five years
	• **Data source:** FHA Single Family Data Warehouse
	• **Unit of measurement:** Loans with specified credit score conditions
	• **Dimension:** Percent
	• **Calculation method:** by age/seasoning of loans, show percentage that have NOT resulted in claim nor are in the process of borrowers losing their homes through short sale, DIL, or foreclosure. We need to be careful to treat a streamline refinance as-if it were a continuation of the original home-purchase loan for this exercise.
	• **Frequency:** Quarterly
	• **Direction**: Increased
	• **Data quality (limitations/advantages of the data):** Data comes from FHA systems and is solid.
	• **Measurement Validation, verification, and improvement of measure:** We will likely see ways to improve this over time.
	• **Sequence**: 4
Metric	*HUD's Housing Counseling Program clients served*
	• **Description:** This measure will track the number of clients counseled through the HUD Housing Counseling program.
	• **Data source:** 9902
	• **Unit of measurement:** Number of clients counseled
	• **Dimension:** Count
	• **Calculation method:** Number of clients counseled as aggregated by agency reporting into 9902.
	• **Frequency:** Quarterly
	• **Direction**: Increased

	<ul><li>**Data quality (limitations/advantages of the data):** The data originate in the Single Family Insurance System-Claims Subsystem, and for convenience are reported from FHA Single Family Housing Enterprise Data Warehouse.</li><li>**Measurement Validation, verification, and improvement of measure:** No data limitations are known to affect this indicator. The loan servicers enter the FHA data, and the FHA monitors the data entry.</li><li>**Sequence:** 5</li></ul>
Metric	*Percentage of housing counseling clients that gain access to resources to improve their housing situation* <ul><li>**Description:** This measure will track the percentage of housing counseling clients who gain access to resources to help them improve their housing situation (e.g., down payment assistance, rental assistance) as a direct result of receiving Housing Counseling Services.</li><li>**Data source:** Revised 9902 to be released October 2014</li><li>**Unit of measurement:** Clients households counseled that gain access to housing finance resources</li><li>**Dimension:** Percentage</li><li>**Calculation method:** Total number of clients that gain access to resources, divided clients counseled.</li><li>**Frequency:** Quarterly</li><li>**Direction:** Increased</li><li>**Data quality (limitations/advantages of the data):** The data originate in the Single Family Insurance System-Claims Subsystem, and for convenience are reported from FHA Single Family Housing Enterprise Data Warehouse</li><li>**Measurement Validation, verification, and improvement of measure:** No data limitations are known to affect this indicator. The loan servicers enter the FHA data, and the FHA monitors the data entry.</li><li>**Sequence:** 6</li></ul>
Strategic Objective 1C	Restore the Federal Housing Administration's financial health, while supporting the housing market recovery and access to mortgage financing.
Metric	*Asset disposition recovery rate* <ul><li>**Description:** This is the net recovery rate that FHA realizes on the sale of distressed assets as a percentage of unpaid loan balance.</li><li>**Data source:** FHA Single Family Data Warehouse</li><li>**Unit of measurement:** Net recovery rate as a percentage of unpaid loan balance of loans that go to claim.</li><li>**Dimension:** Percentage of defaulted unpaid principal balance (UPB)</li><li>**Calculation method:** Standard calculations from our monthly Loan Performance Trends Report.</li><li>**Frequency:** Quarterly</li><li>**Direction:** reduced overall loss rates (increased recovery rates)</li><li>**Data quality (limitations/advantages of the data):** There are timing lags and reporting lags that make this difficult to accurately assess in real time.</li><li>**Measurement Validation, verification, and improvement of measure:** We are constantly reviewing how we calculate net loss and recovery on asset disposition.</li><li>**Sequence:** 7</li></ul>
Metric	*Percentage of modifications resulting in re-defaults within six months of closing* <ul><li>**Description:** This measure will track the percentage of borrowers that become 90 days or more delinquent on their loans within six months of receiving a loan modification/FHA HAMP product.</li></ul>

	<ul><li>**Data source:** FHA Single Family Data Warehouse</li><li>**Unit of measurement:** Borrowers</li><li>**Dimension:** Percentage</li><li>**Calculation method:** For the current month, determine 1) how many loan mods were paid during the previous 6 months and 2) how many are presently 90+ days down. Divide 2) results by 1) results.</li><li>**Frequency:** Monthly</li><li>**Direction:** Decreased</li><li>**Data quality (limitations/advantages of the data):** The data originate in the Single Family Insurance System-Claims Subsystem, and for convenience are reported from FHA Single Family Housing Enterprise Data Warehouse.</li><li>**Measurement Validation, verification, and improvement of measure:** No data limitations are known to affect this indicator. The loan servicers enter the FHA data, and the FHA monitors the data entry.</li><li>**Sequence:** 8</li></ul>
Metric	***Loss mitigation uptake*** <ul><li>**Description:** This is the percentage of permanent loss mitigation actions taken as a percentage of serious delinquencies.</li><li>**Data source:** FHA Single Family Data Warehouse</li><li>**Unit of measurement:** Borrowers</li><li>**Dimension:** Percentage</li><li>**Calculation method**: For the current month, determine 1) how many loan mods were paid during the previous 6 months and 2) how many are presently 90+ days down. Divide 2) results by 1) results.</li><li>**Frequency:** Monthly</li><li>**Direction:** Increased</li><li>**Data quality (limitations/advantages of the data):** For the current month, determine 1) how many loan mods were paid during the previous 6 months and 2) how many are presently 90+ days down. Divide 2) results by 1) results.</li><li>**Measurement Validation, verification, and improvement of measure:** No data limitations are known to affect this indicator. The loan servicers enter the FHA data, and the FHA monitors the data entry.</li><li>**Sequence:** 9</li></ul>
Metric	***Number of FHA insured mortgages benefitting from housing counseling*** <ul><li>**Description:** This is the number of FHA borrowers that receive pre- or post-purchase counseling.</li><li>**Data source:** FHA Single Family Data Warehouse</li><li>**Unit of measurement:** Number of specified mortgages</li><li>**Dimension:** Count</li><li>**Calculation method:** Number of FHA borrowers under specified conditions</li><li>**Frequency:** To be determined after February 2015</li><li>**Direction:** Increased</li><li>**Data quality (limitations/advantages of the data):** To be determined</li><li>**Measurement Validation, verification, and improvement of measure:** No data limitations are known to affect this indicator. The loan servicers enter the FHA data, and the FHA monitors the data entry.</li><li>**Sequence:** 10</li></ul>
Metric	***Capital Reserve Ratio*** <ul><li>**Description:** The capital ratio compares the "economic net worth" of the MMI Fund to the</li></ul>

dollar balance of active, insured loans, at a point in time. Economic net worth is defined as a net asset position, where the present value of expected future revenues and net claim expenses is added to current balance sheet positions. The capital ratio computation is part of an annual valuation of the outstanding portfolio of insured loans at the end of each fiscal year.

- **Data source:** FHA Single Family Data Warehouse Meta Tables.
- **Unit of measurement:** Comparative between net asset position to balance of loans
- **Dimension:** Ratio
- **Calculation method:** The Net Present Value of future cash flows plus capital resources divided by insurance-in-force
- **Frequency:** annual; we will investigate ways of showing on a quarterly basis how the business is actually tracking against the most recent actuarial forecast.
- **Direction:** Increased
- **Data quality (limitations/advantages of the data):** The data originate in the Single Family Insurance System-Claims Subsystem, and for convenience are reported from FHA Single Family Housing Enterprise Data Warehouse.
- **Measurement Validation, verification, and improvement of measure:** No data limitations are known to affect this indicator. The loan servicers enter the FHA data, and the FHA monitors the data entry.
- **Sequence:** 11

Strategic Goal 2	Meet the Need for Quality Affordable Rental Homes
Strategic Objective 2A	Ensure sustainable investments in affordable rental housing.
Metric	*Number of households experiencing "Worst Case Housing Needs"* • **Description:** Long-term series of reports designed to measure the scale of critical housing problems facing very low-income, un-assisted renters • **Data source:** American Housing Survey • **Unit of measurement:** Number of specified households • **Dimension:** Count • **Calculation method:** Biennial survey • **Frequency:** Annual • **Direction:** Downwards • **Data quality (limitations/advantages of the data):** The AHS provides current information on a wide range of housing subjects, including size and composition of the nation's housing inventory, vacancies, fuel usage, physical condition of housing units, characteristics of occupants, equipment breakdowns, home improvements, mortgages and other housing costs, persons eligible for and beneficiaries of assisted housing, home values, and characteristics of recent movers. In addition to these core indicators, the 2013 AHS includes topical supplements on public transportation, emergency and disaster preparedness, community involvement, neighborhood characteristics, and doubled-up households (movers entering and leaving unit). Topical supplements added in 2011 (health and safety hazards, modifications made to assist occupants with disabilities, and energy efficiency) were dropped, but may rotate back into the questionnaire in subsequent surveys. • **Measurement Validation, verification, and improvement of measure:** Current plans call for a complete AHS sample redesign beginning with the 2015 survey. As a result, data from the new sample will not be comparable with those from the previous sample. • **Sequence:** 12
Metric	*Proportion of very-low income renters facing severe rent burdens* • **Description:** • **Data source:** American Community Survey • **Unit of measurement:** Specified renters with rent burdens • **Dimension:** Ratio • **Calculation method:** Annual Surveys

	<ul><li>**Frequency:** Annual</li><li>**Direction:** Downwards</li><li>**Data quality (limitations/advantages of the data):** All data that are based on samples, such as the ACS and the census long-form samples, include a range of uncertainty. Two broad types of error can occur: sampling error and non-sampling error. Non-sampling errors can result from mistakes in how the data are reported or coded, problems in the sampling frame or survey questionnaires, or problems related to nonresponse or interviewer bias. The Census Bureau tries to minimize non-sampling errors by using trained interviewers and by carefully reviewing the survey's sampling methods, data processing techniques, and questionnaire design.</li><li>**Measurement Validation, verification, and improvement of measure:** See above.</li><li>**Sequence:** 13</li></ul>
Metric	*Percentage of rental units built in the preceding four years that had rents below $800*<ul><li>**Description:** These metric tracks the percentage of units built that are affordable for the median renter.</li><li>**Data source:** American Housing Survey</li><li>**Unit of measurement:** Percentage of rental units built that are affordable</li><li>**Dimension:** Percentage</li><li>**Calculation method:** Biennial Surveys</li><li>**Frequency:** Annual</li><li>**Direction:** Increase</li><li>**Data quality (limitations/advantages of the data):):** The AHS provides current information on a wide range of housing subjects, including size and composition of the nation's housing inventory, vacancies, fuel usage, physical condition of housing units, characteristics of occupants, equipment breakdowns, home improvements, mortgages and other housing costs, persons eligible for and beneficiaries of assisted housing, home values, and characteristics of recent movers. In addition to these core indicators, the 2013 AHS includes topical supplements on public transportation, emergency and disaster preparedness, community involvement, neighborhood characteristics, and doubled-up households (movers entering and leaving unit). Topical supplements added in 2011 (health and safety hazards, modifications made to assist occupants with disabilities, and energy efficiency) were dropped, but may rotate back into the questionnaire in subsequent surveys.</li><li>**Measurement Validation, verification, and improvement of measure:** Current plans call for a complete AHS sample redesign beginning with the 2015 survey. As a result, data from the new sample will not be comparable with those from the previous sample.</li><li>**Sequence:** 14</li></ul>
Strategic Objective 2B	Preserve quality affordable rental housing, where it is needed most, by simplifying and aligning the delivery of rental housing programs.
Metric	*Number of families served through HUD rental assistance*<ul><li>**Description:** Total number of families served through HUD rental assistance</li><li>**Data source:** Multiple</li><li>**Unit of measurement:** Families served through HUD rental assistance</li><li>**Dimension:** Count</li><li>**Calculation method:** Total count of rental assistance programs serving families</li><li>**Frequency:** Varied, see below</li><li>**Direction:** Increased</li><li>**Data quality (limitations/advantages of the data):** See submetrics below.</li><li>**Measurement Validation, verification, and improvement of measure:** See submetrics below.</li><li>**Sequence:** 15</li></ul>

Public and Indian Housing

Public Housing

- **Description:** This indicator tracks the number of occupied rental units within PIH's Public Housing stock, which play a significant role in contributing to overall families served by HUD.
- **Data source:** HUD's Inventory Management System/Public and Indian Housing Information Center System
- **Unit of measurement:** Public Housing occupied rental units
- **Dimension:** Count
- **Calculation method:** The Public Housing occupied rental units count is selected from and based on the universe of Public Housing units that are identified as currently under ACC (Annual Contribution Contract) within IMS/PIC. Public Housing units are assigned with a unit category and status to note the nature of use within the program. The count of units within unit statuses are summed to produce the Public Housing occupied rental units count.
- **Frequency:** Quarterly
- **Direction:** Increase
- **Data quality (limitations/advantages of the data):** Public housing agencies self-report the data. Public housing agencies annually certify to the accuracy of the building and unit counts as required by the Office of Capital Improvements. Public housing agencies certify to the accuracy of the data submitted to HUD in the Inventory Management System/Public Housing Information system that the Department uses to calculate the formula for allocating Capital Fund and Operating Fund grants.
- **Measurement Validation, verification, and improvement of measure:** With the annual recertification process, data inconsistencies are identified in the Inventory Management System/Public Housing Information Center system. Public housing agencies correct errors in the data displayed on the Capital Fund Building and Unit Data Certification tab page and the Development Details web page. These data corrections are required before certifying the accuracy of the data for that development. When a public housing agency encounters errors that the public housing agency or field office staff cannot correct, the public housing agency is required to inform the Real Estate Assessment Center Technical Assistance Center Help Desk. This center assigns a Help Ticket number to the public housing agency, and the public housing agency enters the number on the Development Details web page. Finally, the public housing agency must also provide a comment that indicates what data elements are wrong, what the correct data are, and why the data cannot be corrected through the normal procedures.
- **Sequence:** 15a

Tenant Based Rental Assistance Vouchers (TBRA) [HCV]

- **Description:** This indicator tracks the number of occupied rental units within PIH's Housing Choice Vouchers program, including tenant based and Project Based Vouchers. These numbers represent a change from a baseline of 2.2 million units. This data is reported 70 days after the end of the quarter due to data validation processes.
- **Data source:** HUD's Voucher Management System
- **Unit of measurement:** TBRA occupied rental units
- **Dimension:** Count
- **Calculation method:** The Public Housing occupied rental units count is selected from and based on the universe of Public Housing units that are identified as currently under ACC (Annual Contribution Contract) within IMS/PIC. Public Housing units are assigned with a unit category and status to note the nature of use within the program. The count of units within the following unit statuses are summed to produce the Public Housing occupied rental units count:
- **Frequency:** Quarterly
- **Direction:** Increase
- **Data quality (limitations/advantages of the data):** The Voucher Management System

captures information related to the leading and Housing Assistance Payment expenses for the Housing Choice Voucher program. The public housing agencies enter the information, which provides the latest available leading and expense data. The data, therefore, are subject to human (data-entry) error. The Department, however, has instituted "hard edits" for entries in the system.

- **Measurement Validation, verification, and improvement of measure**: A "hard edit" is generated when a public housing agency enters data that are inconsistent with prior months' data input. When a hard edit is generated, a financial analyst reviews the data and, if necessary, contacts the public housing agency to resolve differences. If the issue cannot be resolved successfully, the transaction is rejected and the public housing agency is required to re-enter the correct information. This process provides additional assurance that the reported data are accurate. The Housing Choice Voucher Program uses four other means to ensure the accuracy of the data:

  1. HUD has developed a voucher utilization projection tool, which will enable the Department and public housing agencies to forecast voucher utilization and better manage the Voucher program.

  2. The Housing Choice Voucher Financial Management Division performs data-validation checks of the Voucher Management System data after the monthly database has been submitted to HUD Headquarters for management reporting purposes. Data that appear to be inconsistent with prior months' data are resolved with the public housing agency. Corrections are entered directly into the Voucher Management System to ensure that the data are accurate.

  3. The Public and Indian Housing Quality Assurance Division, using onsite and remote Voucher Management System reviews, validates the data. The division staff reviews source documents on site at the public housing agency to determine if the leasing, Housing Assistance Program expenses, and Net Restricted Assets are consistent with data reported in the Voucher Management System. REAC also compares VMS to FASS data and rejects it if it is materially different.

- **Sequence:** 15b

Office of Native American Programs (ONAP)
- **Description:** This indicator tracks the number of rental units in PIH's Office of Native American Programs (ONAP) housing stock.
- **Data source:** HUD's Voucher Management System
- **Unit of measurement:** ONAP-occupied rental units
- **Dimension:** Count
- **Calculation method:** ONAP occupied rental units count is selected from and based on the universe of Public Housing units that are identified as currently under ACC (Annual Contribution Contract) within IMS/PIC. Public Housing units are assigned with a unit category and status to note the nature of use within the program. The count of units within the following unit statuses are summed to produce the ONAP occupied rental units count.
- **Frequency:** Quarterly
- **Direction:** Increase
- **Data quality (limitations/advantages of the data):** The Voucher Management System captures information related to the leading and Housing Assistance Payment expenses for the Housing Choice Voucher program. The public housing agencies enter the information, which provides the latest available leading and expense data. The data, therefore, are subject to human (data-entry) error. The Department, however, has instituted "hard edits" for entries in the system.
- **Measurement Validation, verification, and improvement of measure:** A "hard edit" is generated when a public housing agency enters data that are inconsistent with prior months' data input. When a hard edit is generated, a financial analyst reviews the data and, if

necessary, contacts the public housing agency to resolve differences. If the issue cannot be resolved successfully, the transaction is rejected and the public housing agency is required to re-enter the correct information. This process provides additional assurance that the reported data are accurate.

- **Sequence:** 15c

Mainstream Vouchers

- **Description:** Mainstream program vouchers enable families having a person with disabilities to lease affordable private housing of their choice. Mainstream program vouchers also assist persons with disabilities who often face difficulties in locating suitable and accessible housing on the private market.
- **Description:** This indicator tracks the number of occupied rental units within PIH's Housing Choice Vouchers program, including tenant based and Project Based Vouchers. These numbers represent a change from a baseline of 2.2 million units. This data is reported 70 days after the end of the quarter due to data validation processes.
- **Data source:** HUD's Voucher Management System
- **Unit of measurement:** TBRA occupied rental units
- **Dimension:** Count
- **Calculation method:** The Public Housing occupied rental units count is selected from and based on the universe of Public Housing units that are identified as currently under ACC (Annual Contribution Contract) within IMS/PIC. Public Housing units are assigned with a unit category and status to note the nature of use within the program. The count of units within the following unit statuses are summed to produce the Public Housing occupied rental units count:
- **Frequency:** Quarterly
- **Direction:** Increase
- **Data quality (limitations/advantages of the data):** The Voucher Management System captures information related to the leading and Housing Assistance Payment expenses for the Housing Choice Voucher program. The public housing agencies enter the information, which provides the latest available leading and expense data. The data, therefore, are subject to human (data-entry) error. The Department, however, has instituted "hard edits" for entries in the system.
- **Measurement Validation, verification, and improvement of measure**: A "hard edit" is generated when a public housing agency enters data that are inconsistent with prior months' data input. When a hard edit is generated, a financial analyst reviews the data and, if necessary, contacts the public housing agency to resolve differences. If the issue cannot be resolved successfully, the transaction is rejected and the public housing agency is required to re-enter the correct information. This process provides additional assurance that the reported data are accurate. The Housing Choice Voucher Program uses four other means to ensure the accuracy of the data:
  1. HUD has developed a voucher utilization projection tool, which will enable the Department and public housing agencies to forecast voucher utilization and better manage the Voucher program.
  2. The Housing Choice Voucher Financial Management Division performs data-validation checks of the Voucher Management System data after the monthly database has been submitted to HUD Headquarters for management reporting purposes. Data that appear to be inconsistent with prior months' data are resolved with the public housing agency. Corrections are entered directly into the Voucher Management System to ensure that the data are accurate.
  3. The Public and Indian Housing Quality Assurance Division, using onsite and remote Voucher Management System reviews, validates the data. The division staff reviews source documents on site at the public housing agency to determine if the leasing, Housing Assistance Program expenses, and Net Restricted Assets are consistent with data reported in

the Voucher Management System. REAC also compares VMS to FASS data and rejects it if it is materially different.

- **Sequence:** 15d

PIH Moderate Rehabilitation

- **Description:** The moderate rehabilitation program provides project-based rental assistance for low income families. The program was repealed in 1991 and no new projects are authorized for development. Assistance is limited to properties previously rehabilitated pursuant to a housing assistance payments (HAP) contract between an owner and a Public Housing Agency (PHA).
- **Data source:** Each year, public housing agencies provide data to the Public and Indian Housing field offices, Section 5 ▪ Additional Information 63 including which Moderate Rehabilitation contracts will be renewed. The field offices calculate renewal rents
- and forward all data to the Financial Management Center, which confirms the data and also calculates and requests total required renewal and replacement funding. After funding has been received, the Financial Management Center obligates and disburses funding for Moderate Rehabilitation Renewals or Replacement vouchers with Housing Choice Vouchers funds.
- **Unit of measurement:** Specified rental occupied units
- **Dimension:** Count
- **Calculation method:**
- **Frequency:** Quarterly
- **Direction:** Increase
- **Data quality (limitations/advantages of the data):** Timeliness and validity of data are dependent on multiple entities, including the Moderate Rehabilitation project owners, Public and Indian Housing field offices, and the Financial Management Center. It is primarily a detailed, time-consuming, manual process.
- **Measurement Validation, verification, and improvement of measure:** The Financial Management Center reviews the data provided by the field offices and follows-up on incorrect or suspect data before submitting funding requests. A Financial Management Center division director or team leader must approve funding obligation and disbursement. The Office of Housing Voucher Programs is currently working to develop a more streamlined and automated process to validate and improve the validation.
- **Sequence:** 15e

Housing

Project-Based Rental Assistance (PBRA) [Section 8]

- **Description:** This sub-metric tracks the number of families receiving rental assistance through the Section 8 PBRA program
- **Data source:** Tenant Rental Assistance Certificate System (TRACS) and Integrated Real Estate Management System (iREMS)
- **Unit of measurement:** Families receiving rental assistance through the Section 8 Project-Based Rental Assistance program
- **Dimension:** Count
- **Calculation method: Total count of units receiving rental assistance through the Section 8 Project-Based Rental Assistance program**
- **Frequency:** Quarterly
- **Direction:** Flat
- **Data quality (limitations/advantages of the data):** The Tenant Rental Assistance Certificate System (TRACS) has more than 6,000 business rules to ensure data validation. The applications are working with clean, accurate, and meaningful data. Data fields are required

for property and project management purposes. These systems serve two primary customers: HUD staff and business partners called performance-based contract administrators.

- **Measurement Validation, verification, and improvement of measure:** The system business rules and operating procedures are defined in HUD Occupancy Handbook 4350.3; HUD's IT system security protocols; and financial requirements established in the Office of Management and Budget's Circular A-127. Often referenced as validation rules, these business rules check for data accuracy, meaningfulness, and security of access logic and controls. The primary data element for the Tenant Rental Assistance Certificate System is the HUD 50059 tenant certification, which originates from owner/agents, performance-based contract administrators, and traditional contract administrators. HUD's 50059 transmissions are processed via secure system access and a predetermined system script. Invalid data are identified by an error code and are returned to the sender with a descriptive message and procedures to correct the error. This electronic process approximates that of the paper Form HUD 50059. The Tenant Rental Assistance Certificate System edits every field, according to the HUD rental assistance program policies.
- **Sequence:** 15f

Rental Assistance Payments (RAP)
- **Description:** This sub-metric tracks the number of families receiving rental assistance through the Rental Assistance Payment (RAP) program
- **Data source:** Tenant Rental Assistance Certificate System (TRACS) and Integrated Real Estate Management System (iREMS)
- **Unit of measurement:** Families receiving rental assistance through the Rental Assistance Payment (RAP) program
- **Dimension: Count**
- **Calculation method: Total count of units receiving assistance through the Rental Assistance Payment (RAP) program**
- **Frequency: Quarterly**
- **Direction: Decreasing**
- **Data quality (limitations/advantages of the data):** The Tenant Rental Assistance Certificate System (TRACS) has more than 6,000 business rules to ensure data validation. The applications are working with clean, accurate, and meaningful data. Data fields are required for property and project management purposes.
- **Measurement Validation, verification, and improvement of measure: :** The system business rules and operating procedures are defined in HUD Occupancy Handbook 4350.3; HUD's IT system security protocols; and financial requirements established in the Office of Management and Budget's Circular A-127. Often referenced as validation rules, these business rules check for data accuracy, meaningfulness, and security of access logic and controls. The primary data element for the Tenant Rental Assistance Certificate System is the HUD 50059 tenant certification, which originates from owner/agents,. HUD's 50059 transmissions are processed via secure system access and a predetermined system script. Invalid data are identified by an error code and are returned to the sender with a descriptive message and procedures to correct the error. This electronic process approximates that of the paper Form HUD 50059. The Tenant Rental Assistance Certificate System edits every field, according to the HUD rental assistance program policies.
- **Sequence:** 15g

Rent Supplement
- **Description:** This sub-metric tracks the number of families receiving rental assistance through the Rent Supplement (SUP) program
- **Data source: :** Tenant Rental Assistance Certificate System (TRACS) and Integrated Real

Estate Management System (iREMS)

- **Unit of measurement:** Families receiving rental assistance through Rent Supplement (SUP) program
- **Dimension: Count**
- **Calculation method: Total count of units receiving assistance through the Rent Supplement (SUP) program**
- **Frequency: Quarterly**
- **Direction: Decreasing**
- **Data quality (limitations/advantages of the data):** The Tenant Rental Assistance Certificate System (TRACS) has more than 6,000 business rules to ensure data validation. The applications are working with clean, accurate, and meaningful data. Data fields are required for property and project management purposes.
- **Measurement Validation, verification, and improvement of measure:** The system business rules and operating procedures are defined in HUD Occupancy Handbook 4350.3; HUD's IT system security protocols; and financial requirements established in the Office of Management and Budget's Circular A-127. Often referenced as validation rules, these business rules check for data accuracy, meaningfulness, and security of access logic and controls. The primary data element for the Tenant Rental Assistance Certificate System is the HUD 50059 tenant certification, which originates from owner/agents. HUD's 50059 transmissions are processed via secure system access and a predetermined system script. Invalid data are identified by an error code and are returned to the sender with a descriptive message and procedures to correct the error. This electronic process approximates that of the paper Form HUD 50059. The Tenant Rental Assistance Certificate System edits every field, according to the HUD rental assistance program policies.
- **Sequence:** 15h

Project Rental Assistance Contract (Sections 202 Elderly and 811 Persons with Disabilities) [PRAC 202/811]

- **Description:** This sub-metric tracks the number of families receiving rental assistance through the 202/811 Project Rental Assistance program.
- **Data source:** Tenant Rental Assistance Certificate System (TRACS) and Integrated Real Estate Management System (iREMS)
- **Unit of measurement:** Families receiving rental assistance through the 202/811 Project Rental Assistance program
- **Dimension: Count**
- **Calculation method: Total count of units receiving assistance through a 202/811 PRAC**
- **Frequency:** Quarterly
- **Direction:** Increasing
- **Data quality (limitations/advantages of the data):** The Tenant Rental Assistance Certificate System (TRACS) has more than 6,000 business rules to ensure data validation. The applications are working with clean, accurate, and meaningful data. Data fields are required for property and project management purposes.
- **Measurement Validation, verification, and improvement of measure:** The system business rules and operating procedures are defined in HUD Occupancy Handbook 4350.3; HUD's IT system security protocols; and financial requirements established in the Office of Management and Budget's Circular A-127. Often referenced as validation rules, these business rules check for data accuracy, meaningfulness, and security of access logic and controls. The primary data element for the Tenant Rental Assistance Certificate System is the HUD 50059 tenant certification, which originates from owner/agents. HUD's 50059 transmissions are processed via secure system access and a predetermined system script. Invalid data are identified by an error code and are returned to the sender with a descriptive

message and procedures to correct the error. This electronic process approximates that of the paper Form HUD 50059. The Tenant Rental Assistance Certificate System edits every field, according to the HUD rental assistance program policies.

- **Sequence:** 15i

Insured Tax-Exempt/Low-Income Tax Credit (LIHTC)
- **Description:** The LIHTC Program is an indirect Federal subsidy used to finance the development of affordable rental housing for low-income households.
- **Data source:** Office of Housing Development Management Action Plan goals SharePoint site
- **Unit of measurement:** Number of Tax Credits
- **Dimension:** Count
- **Calculation method:**
- **Frequency:** Quarterly
- **Direction:** Increased
- **Data quality (limitations/advantages of the data):** Complete new LIHTCH/TE units are posed on the SharePoint site based on data provided by the HUD Project Managers who have worked on these projects. The data are judged to be reliable for this measure.
- **Measurement Validation, verification, and improvement of measure:** HUD field staff provide the data which is reviewed and verified by Multifamily Hub and Headquarters staff.
- **Sequence:** 15j

202, 236 and 221d3 BMIR
- **Description:** Count of units covered by old 202 direct loans, insured under Section 236, receiving interest reduction payments (IRP), or insured under Section 223(d)(3)BMIR.
- **Data source:** Multifamily Portfolio Reporting Database (MPRD)
- **Unit of measurement:** Number of families living in units subsidized by the old 202, 236, IRP, and BMIR programs
- **Dimension:** Count
- **Calculation method:** Count of units
- **Frequency:** Quarterly
- **Direction:** Decreasing (as mortgages mature)
- **Data quality (limitations/advantages of the data):** All of these units are assumed to be occupied. There is no assurance that this assumption is correct.
- **Measurement Validation, verification, and improvement of measure:** The number of units per project in the MPRD comes from iREMS and has been validated multiple times by project managers in field asset management against source documents.
- **Sequence:** 15k

Community Planning and Development

HOME Occupied Rental Units

- **Description:** HOME funds may be used for the acquisition, new construction or rehabilitation of affordable rental housing
- **Data source:** IDIS
- **Unit of measurement:** Occupied Rental Units
- **Dimension:** Count
- **Calculation method:** Data is derived from grantee accomplishments reported by HOME grantees in the Integrated Disbursement and Information System.
- **Frequency:** Quarterly

- **Direction:** Increased
- **Data quality (limitations/advantages of the data):** Data reliability has been enhanced by the re-engineering of the system at the end of FY 2009 into FY 2010.
- **Measurement Validation, verification, and improvement of measure:** When monitoring grantees, Community Planning and Development field staff verifies program data.
- **Sequence:** 15m

Community Development Block Grants—Disaster Relief (CDBG-DR)

- **Description:** The number of rental units
- **Data source:** DRGR
- **Unit of measurement:** # of Low and moderate income renter households
- **Dimension:** Count
- **Calculation method:** Data is derived from CDBG-DR Sandy grantee projections reported in DRGR
- **Frequency:** Quarterly
- **Direction:** Increase
- **Data quality (limitations/advantages of the data):** Sandy grantees are still providing projections
- **Measurement Validation, verification, and improvement of measure:** Sandy grantees are still providing projections
- **Sequence:** 15n

Housing Opportunities for Persons with Aids (HOPWA)

- **Description:** The HOPWA program collects performance outcomes on housing stability, access to care, and prevention of homelessness.
- **Data source:** Integrated Disbursement and Information System (IDIS)
- **Unit of measurement:** Specified persons receiving assistance
- **Dimension:** Count
- **Calculation method:** These performance reports are collected by grantees
- **Frequency:** Annually
- **Direction:** Increased
- **Data quality (limitations/advantages of the data):** Data are reported by formula and competitive grantees through the Consolidated Annual Performance and Evaluation Report and the Annual Progress Report, respectively. These reports reflect annual data collection with limited use of information management technology systems, pending further upgrades. These performance reports are completed by grantees provide the program with insights into client demographics, expenditures for eligible activities, and the number of households served. At this time, the program does not have a client-level data system that provides site-specific information on performance outcomes. Pending enhancements to IDIS, however, will help support data quality and reduce the grantees' burden.
- **Measurement Validation, verification, and improvement of measure:** Performance reporting information is reviewed by HOPWA technical assistance providers and recorded in grant profiles and national summaries on the program's website (HUDHRE.info). HUD guidance and technical assistance assists grantees in verifying data quality and completing reports.
- **Sequence:** 15o

McKinney-Vento Homeless Assistance Units

	<ul><li>**Description:** The number of occupied rental units provided through the McKinney-Vento Act</li><li>**Data source:** HIC</li><li>**Unit of measurement:** Occupied rental units for specified people</li><li>**Dimension:** Count</li><li>**Calculation method:** Number of McKinney-Vento funded rental units</li><li>**Frequency:** Quarterly</li><li>**Direction:** Increased</li><li>**Data quality (limitations/advantages of the data):** CoCs apply for funding for McKinney-Vento rental assistance</li><li>**Measurement Validation, verification, and improvement of measure:**</li><li>**Sequence:** 15p</li></ul> HOME TBRA <ul><li>**Description:** For tenants with incomes at or below 80 percent of area median income.</li><li>**Data source:** IDIS</li><li>**Unit of measurement:** Households assisted with TBRA</li><li>**Dimension:** Count</li><li>**Calculation method:** Data is derived from grantee accomplishments reported by HOME grantees in the Integrated Disbursement and Information System.</li><li>**Frequency:** Quarterly</li><li>**Direction:** Increased</li><li>**Data quality (limitations/advantages of the** data): Current data systems do not capture the length of time or type of assistance (e.g. security deposit) provided to households.</li><li>**Measurement Validation, verification, and improvement of measure:** : When monitoring grantees, Community Planning and Development field staff verifies program data. For FY 2014, presentation of this data is being revised.</li><li>**Sequence:** 15q</li></ul>
Metric	***Number of units converted using the Rental Assistance Demonstration (RAD)*** <ul><li>**Description:** Number of units converted using the Rental Assistance Demonstration Program</li><li>**Data source:** OAHP data systems</li><li>**Unit of measurement:** Units converted through RAD</li><li>**Dimension:** Count</li><li>**Calculation method:** Total units counted through RAD</li><li>**Frequency:** Quarterly</li><li>**Direction:** Increased</li><li>**Data quality (limitations/advantages of the data): The data is considered to be accurate and reliable.**</li><li>**Measurement Validation, verification, and improvement of measure:** The data is entered and validated by OAHP staff.</li><li>**Sequence:** 16</li></ul>
Metric	***Housing Choice Voucher utilization rate*** <ul><li>**Description:** Percentage of Housing Choice Vouchers used</li><li>**Data source:** VMS</li><li>**Unit of measurement:** Vouchers utilized</li><li>**Dimension:** Percentage</li><li>**Calculation method:** Vouchers utilized divided by total vouchers</li><li>**Frequency:** Quarterly</li><li>**Direction:** Increased</li><li>**Data quality (limitations/advantages of the data):** The Voucher Management System</li></ul>

	captures information related to the leading and Housing Assistance Payment expenses for the Housing Choice Voucher program. The public housing agencies enter the information, which provides the latest available leading and expense data. The data, therefore, are subject to human (data-entry) error. The Department, however, has instituted "hard edits" for entries in the system.
	• **Measurement Validation, verification, and improvement of measure:** A "hard edit" is generated when a public housing agency enters data that are inconsistent with prior months' data input. When a hard edit is generated, a financial analyst reviews the data and, if necessary, contacts the public housing agency to resolve differences. If the issue cannot be resolved successfully, the transaction is rejected and the public housing agency is required to re-enter the correct information. This process provides additional assurance that the reported data are accurate. The Housing Choice Voucher Program uses four other means to ensure the accuracy of the data:
	1. HUD has developed a voucher utilization projection tool, which will enable the Department and public housing agencies to forecast voucher utilization and better manage the Voucher program.
	2. The Housing Choice Voucher Financial Management Division performs data-validation checks of the Voucher Management System data after the monthly database has been submitted to HUD Headquarters for management reporting purposes. Data that appear to be inconsistent with prior months' data are resolved with the public housing agency. Corrections are entered directly into the Voucher Management System to ensure that the data are accurate.
	3. The Public and Indian Housing Quality Assurance Division, using onsite and remote Voucher Management System reviews, validates the data. The division staff reviews source documents on site at the public housing agency to determine if the leasing, Housing Assistance Program expenses, and Net Restricted Assets are consistent with data reported in the Voucher Management System. REAC also compares VMS to FASS data and rejects it if it is materially different.
	• **Sequence:** 17
Metric	*Number of units managed under the uniform asset management model*
	• **Description:** Units managed through the uniform asset management model
	• **Data source:** TBD
	• **Unit of measurement:** Units managed through specified model
	• **Dimension:** Count
	• **Calculation method:** Total amount of units managed through UAM model
	• **Frequency: Quarterly**
	• **Direction: Increased**
	• **Data quality (limitations/advantages of the data):**
	• **Measurement Validation, verification, and improvement of measure:**
	• **Sequence:** 18
Metric	*Number of inspections saved through inspection sharing*
	• **Description:** Number of inspections saved through inspection sharing
	• **Data source:** Manual tracking system (SharePoint)
	• **Unit of measurement:** Inspections saved through inspection sharing
	• **Dimension:** Count
	• **Calculation method:** For each property enrolled in the pilot within each year, inspections saved are calculated by taking the sum of inspections that would have taken place per federal programmatic requirements and subtracting the number of physical inspections that have actually taken place, with one inspection ideally serving all needs. The complete metrics is the count of inspections saved for each property is summed with all pilot properties enrolled for

that year.

- **Frequency:** Annually (tracking only)
- **Direction:** Increased
- **Data quality (limitations/advantages of the data):** The Physical Inspection Alignment pilot utilizes several combined sources of information, including HUD-REAC systems, state HFA reports, and USDA-RD reports, to create a baseline of properties to be enrolled in and inspected as part of the alignment pilot. Although some information does come directly from systems (PASS, IREMS), and is combined utilizing SQL queries and Access databases, there is manual manipulation of tracking system data by pilot team staff that is unavoidable, as sources for this information are not located elsewhere. Because no defined system exists, nor are there areas to enter relevant pilot data into preexisting systems, manual errors are a risk.
- **Measurement Validation, verification, and improvement of measure:** Inspections completed by REAC inspectors or contracted inspectors are validated per normal processes—the completion of inspections is systematic and relatively error-free. Inspections completed by HFA partners are validated through other means, but the actual completion of an inspection is verified and maintained in our manual tracking system.
- **Sequence:** 19

Metric	*Public Housing occupancy rate*
	<ul><li>**Description:** Occupancy rate in public housing</li><li>**Data source:** IMS/PIC</li><li>**Unit of measurement:** Percentage of occupied public housing units</li><li>**Dimension:** Percentage</li><li>**Calculation method:** The APG Occupancy Rate is calculated using the following methodology: Total of Public Housing occupied rental units + (Total Standing ACC Units – Total Unihabitable Units) This count is the sum of units occupied by assisted tenants, units occupied by non-assisted tenants, and Special Use units. Total Standing ACC Units, refers to the number of standing (i.e. not removed) units under Annual Contributions Contracts with HUD. The number of Uninhabitable Units refers ti ACC units that are vacant and approved for removal from inventory.</li><li>**Frequency:** Quarterly</li><li>**Direction:** Increased</li><li>**Data quality (limitations/advantages of the data):** The Public Housing occupancy rate faces the same limitations as the "Public Housing occupied rental units" measure. However, the rate may also fluctuate per the changing denominator of ACC units, while retaining the same count of Public Housing occupied rental units.</li><li>**Measurement Validation, verification, and improvement of measure:** The Public Housing occupancy rate faces the same limitations as the "Public Housing occupied rental units"</li><li>**Sequence:** 20</li></ul>
Metric	*Project Based Rental Assistance (PBRA) occupancy rate*
	<ul><li>**Description:** Percentage of units occupied for PBRA</li><li>**Data source: Data source:** Tenant Rental Assistance Certificate System (TRACS) and Integrated Real Estate Management System (iREMS)</li><li>**Unit of measurement:** Percent PBRA units occupied</li><li>**Dimension: Percentage**</li><li>**Calculation method:** Occupied Units divided by Total Units</li><li>**Frequency:** Quarterly</li><li>**Direction:** Flat</li></ul>

- **Data quality (limitations/advantages of the data):** The Tenant Rental Assistance Certificate System (TRACS) has more than 6,000 business rules to ensure data validation. The applications are working with clean, accurate, and meaningful data. Data fields are required for property and project management purposes.
- **Measurement Validation, verification, and improvement of measure:** The system business rules and operating procedures are defined in HUD Occupancy Handbook 4350.3; HUD's IT system security protocols; and financial requirements established in the Office of Management and Budget's Circular A-127. Often referenced as validation rules, these business rules check for data accuracy, meaningfulness, and security of access logic and controls. The primary data element for the Tenant Rental Assistance Certificate System is the HUD 50059 tenant certification, which originates from owner/agents, performance-based contract administrators, and traditional contract administrators. HUD's 50059 transmissions are processed via secure system access and a predetermined system script. Invalid data are identified by an error code and are returned to the sender with a descriptive message and procedures to correct the error. This electronic process approximates that of the paper Form HUD 50059. The Tenant Rental Assistance Certificate System edits every field, according to the HUD rental assistance program policies.
- **Sequence: 21**

Strategic Goal 3	Use Housing as a Platform to Improve Quality of Life
Strategic Objective 3A	End homelessness for Veterans, people experiencing chronic homelessness, families, youth and children.
Metric	*Total homeless Veterans temporarily living in shelters or transitional housing* - **Description:** Total homeless Veterans temporarily living in shelters or transitional housing - **Data source:** PIT - **Unit of measurement:** Homeless Veterans in specified situation on a single night in January each year - **Dimension:** Count - **Calculation method:** A count of homeless persons a single night in January each year - **Frequency:** Annual - **Direction:** Increased - **Data quality (limitations/advantages of the data):** HUD establishes Point-in-Time (PIT) guidance annually that states the minimum amount of data that all CoCs must collect and report to HUD as part of its PIT Count. There are additional reporting tools that provide guidance on HUD's reporting requirements and standards. - **Measurement Validation, verification, and improvement of measure:** When CoCs submit their data in the HDX there are also several validations in HDX itself to ensure consistency in reporting. After the data is submitted HUD's contractors analyze the data again and call communities if there are further discrepancies that need to be explained or corrected. - **Sequence: 22**
Metric	*Total Veterans living on the streets, experiencing homelessness* - **Description:** Total Veterans living on the streets, experiencing homelessness - **Data source:** PIT - **Unit of measurement:** Homeless Veterans in specified situation on a single night in January each year - **Dimension:** Count - **Calculation method:** A count of homeless persons a single night in January each year - **Frequency:** Annual - **Direction:** Increased - **Data quality (limitations/advantages of the data):** HUD establishes Point-in-Time (PIT) guidance annually that states the minimum amount of data that all CoCs must collect and

	report to HUD as part of its PIT Count. There are additional reporting tools that provide guidance on HUD's reporting requirements and standards. • **Measurement Validation, verification, and improvement of measure:** When CoCs submit their data in the HDX there are also several validations in HDX itself to ensure consistency in reporting. After the data is submitted HUD's contractors analyze the data again and call communities if there are further discrepancies that need to be explained or corrected. • **Sequence:** 23
Metric	***Veterans placed in permanent housing*** • **Description:** Total number of Veterans housed permanently • **Data source:** Veteran's Affairs Homeless Registry, PIC • **Unit of measurement:** Specified persons • **Dimension:** Count • **Calculation method:** Number of unique Veterans who obtain permanent housing divided by the number of placements • **Frequency:** Quarterly • **Direction:** Increase • **Data quality (limitations/advantages of the data):** CoCs apply for funding for permanent supportive housing for Veterans • **Measurement Validation, verification, and improvement of measure:** HUD staff review each project carefully to ensure the project complies with HUD requirements and reviews the application carefully to verify that the data in the application is accurate • **Sequence:** 24
Metric	***Homeless Veterans served with transitional housing through Continuum of Care resources*** • **Description:** Homeless Veterans served through CoC transitional housing programs • **Data source:** ESNAPS • **Unit of measurement:** Specified individuals • **Dimension:** Count • **Calculation method:** HUD's CoC grant recipients are required to report on their grants 90 days after the grant's operating end date. HUD aggregates the data for an entire year's worth of data. • **Frequency:** Annually • **Direction:** • **Data quality (limitations/advantages of the data):** HUD provides programming specifications to CoCs and grant recipients that are then used by the HMIS programmers. This creates consistency and avoids error. Data is then submitted to HUD via ESNAPS. ESNAPS has several data validations also to ensure consistency. • **Measurement Validation, verification, and improvement of measure:** HUD staff review each project carefully to ensure the project complies with HUD requirements and reviews the application carefully to verify that the data in the application is accurate. • **Sequence:** 25
Metric	***Homeless Veterans served with permanent supportive housing through Continuum of Care resources*** • **Description:** Homeless Veterans served through CoC permanent supported housing programs • **Data source:** ESNAPS • **Unit of measurement:** Count • **Dimension:** Homeless Veterans served in specified manner • **Calculation method:** HUD's CoC grant recipients are required to report on their grants 90 days after the grant's operating end date. HUD aggregates the data for an entire year's worth of data.

	- **Frequency:** Annual - **Direction:** Increase - **Data quality (limitations/advantages of the data):** HUD's CoC grant recipients are required to report on their grants 90 days after the grant's operating end date. HUD aggregates the data for an entire year's worth of data. - **Measurement Validation, verification, and improvement of measure:** HUD provides programming specifications to CoCs and grant recipients that are then used by the HMIS programmers. This creates consistency and avoids error. Data is then submitted to HUD via ESNAPS. ESNAPS has several data validations also to ensure consistency. - **Sequence:** 26
Metric	**_Individuals experiencing chronic homelessness_** - **Description:** Number of chronically homeless individuals - **Data source:** HDX - **Unit of measurement:** Specified individuals - **Dimension:** Count - **Calculation method:** Each CoC is required to conduct an annual sheltered count and an unsheltered count every other year. This data is aggregated and reported for this metric. - **Frequency:** Annually - **Direction:** Decrease - **Data quality (limitations/advantages of the data):** HUD establishes Point-in-Time (PIT) guidance annually that states the minimum amount of data that all CoCs must collect and report to HUD as part of its PIT Count. There are additional reporting tools that provide guidance on HUD's reporting requirements and standards. - **Measurement Validation, verification, and improvement of measure:** When CoCs submit their data in the HDX there are also several validations in HDX itself to ensure consistency in reporting. After the data is submitted HUD's contractors analyze the data again and call communities if there are further discrepancies that need to be explained or corrected. - **Sequence:** 27
Metric	**_Number and percentage of Permanent Supportive Housing beds targeted to individuals experiencing chronic homelessness_** - **Description:** Permanent Supportive Housing beds for chronically homeless - **Data source:** ESNAPS - **Unit of measurement:** Beds for specified individuals - **Dimension:** Count and Percentage - **Calculation method:** HUD conducts an annual competition for CoC Program funding. HUD is continuing to encourage CoCs to use new and reallocated funds to create new permanent supportive housing units for the chronically homeless. This measure reflects the sum of all beds/units funded in the competition that must be dedicated to serve the chronically homeless. - **Frequency:** Annually - **Direction:** Increase - **Data quality (limitations/advantages of the data):** CoCs apply for funding for new permanent supportive housing, with dedicated beds for the chronically homeless. - **Measurement Validation, verification, and improvement of measure:** HUD staff review each project carefully to ensure the project complies with HUD requirements and reviews the application carefully to verify that the data in the application is accurate. - **Sequence:** 28
Metric	**_Families experiencing homelessness_** - **Description:** Number of Families experiencing homelessness - **Data source:** HDX

	• **Unit of measurement:** Specified groups • **Dimension:** Count • **Calculation method:** Each CoC is required to conduct an annual sheltered count and an unsheltered count every other year. This data is aggregated and reported for this metric. • **Frequency:** Annually • **Direction:** Decrease • **Data quality (limitations/advantages of the data):** HUD establishes Point-in-Time (PIT) guidance annually that states the minimum amount of data that all CoCs must collect and report to HUD as part of its PIT Count. There are additional reporting tools that provide guidance on HUD's reporting requirements and standards. • **Measurement Validation, verification, and improvement of measure:** When CoCs submit their data in the HDX there are also several validations in HDX itself to ensure consistency in reporting. After the data is submitted HUD's contractors analyze the data again and call communities if there are further discrepancies that need to be explained or corrected. • **Sequence:** 29
Metric	***Number and percentage of admissions of new homeless families into HUD-assisted Housing*** • **Description:** Admissions of new homeless households into Public Housing • **Data source:** PIC • **Unit of measurement:** New Homeless Admissions • **Dimension:** Count and Percentage • **Calculation method:** Number of families admitted into HUD-assisted housing • **Frequency:** Quarterly • **Direction:** Increased • **Data quality (limitations/advantages of the data):** Public housing agencies self-report the data. Based on a review of PIC reporting on line 4C (homeless at admission) of the Form 50058, PIH found that some PHAs were not reporting in this field accurately, or were reporting "no" for all applicants, whether homeless or not. • **Measurement Validation, verification, and improvement of measure:** PIH issued guidance in the form of Notice PIH 2013-15 to help correct the data quality issue. • **Sequence:** 30a • **Description:** Admissions of new homeless households into HUD-assisted Multifamily units • **Data source:** TRACs • **Unit of measurement:** New Homeless Admissions • **Dimension:** Count • **Calculation method:** Number of families admitted into HUD-assisted housing • **Frequency:** Quarterly • **Direction:** Increasing • **Data quality (limitations/advantages of the data):** Data will be collected beginning in late 2014. Some period of time will be needed to improve the quality of data collection, identify and resolve problems, and to establish baselines. • **Measurement Validation, verification, and improvement of measure:** • **Sequence:** 30b
	Percentage of Emergency Solutions Grant dollars dedicated to Rapid Rehousing for homeless families • **Description:** Percentage of specified grant dollars for Rapid Rehousing of homeless families • **Data source:** IDIS • **Unit of measurement: Grant Dollars** • **Dimension: Percentage** • **Calculation method:** Each year, HUD allocates funding to ESG through a formula grant. HUD is encouraging ESG recipients to use funding to rapid rehouse its participants. HUD will

	look at the percent of its total ESG funds that are expended on RRH activities. • **Frequency:** Annually • **Direction:** Increase • **Data quality (limitations/advantages of the data):** Each year, HUD allocates funding to ESG through a formula grant. HUD is encouraging ESG recipients to use funding to rapid rehouse its participants. • **Measurement Validation, verification, and improvement of measure:** HUD will look at the percent of its total ESG funds that are expended on RRH activities. • **Sequence:** 31
Strategic Objective 3B	Promote advancements in economic prosperity for residents of HUD-assisted housing.
Metric	*Percentage of participants enrolled in the Family Self Sufficiency program that have increased wages* • **Description:** Percent of participants enrolled in FSS program with positive wages • **Data source:** PIH systems • **Unit of measurement:** • **Dimension:** Percentage • **Calculation method:** Percentage of individuals enrolled in FSS with increased wages divided by total participants • **Frequency:** • **Direction:** • **Data quality (limitations/advantages of the data):** • **Measurement Validation, verification, and improvement of measure:** • **Sequence:** 32
Metric	*Percentage of Section 3 Residents hired, of total hiring that occurs as a result of Section 3 covered HUD funding* • **Description:** Percent of Section 3 Residents hired • **Data source:** Section 3 60002 Reporting System • **Unit of measurement:** Specified individuals hired • **Dimension:** Percentage • **Calculation method:** Number of Section 3 residents hired divided by total of all new hires for all agencies that reported during the period • **Frequency:** Annual • **Direction:** Increase • **Data quality (limitations/advantages of the data):** Recipients of HUD funding enter the data for their programs so it is dependent on their understanding of Section 3 and their accuracy. • **Measurement Validation, verification, and improvement of measure:** Sample auditing will be done • **Sequence:** 33
Metric	*Percentage of total dollar amount of construction contracts awarded to Section 3 businesses by covered HUD funding* • **Description:** Percent of total dollar amount of construction contracts awarded to Section 3 businesses by covered HUD funding • **Data source:** Section 3 60002 Reporting System • **Unit of measurement:** Specified dollars used • **Dimension:** Percentage • **Calculation method:** Dollars awarded to Section 3 businesses for construction divided by the total dollars awarded to Section 3 businesses • **Frequency:** Annual • **Direction:** Increase • **Data quality (limitations/advantages of the data):** Recipients of HUD funding enter the data for their programs so it is dependent on their understanding of Section 3 and their accuracy.

	• **Measurement Validation, verification, and improvement of measure:** Sample auditing will be done • **Sequence:** 34
Metric	*Percentage of total dollar amount of non-construction contracts awarded to Section 3 businesses by covered HUD funding* • **Description:** Percent of total dollar amount of non-construction contracts awarded to Section 3 businesses by covered HUD funding • **Data source:** Section 3 60002 Reporting System • **Unit of measurement:** Specified dollars used • **Dimension:** Percentage • **Calculation method:** Dollars awarded to Section 3 businesses for non-construction divided by the total the dollars awarded to Section 3 businesses • **Frequency:** Annual • **Direction:** Increase • **Data quality (limitations/advantages of the data):** Recipients of HUD funding enter the data for their programs so it is dependent on their understanding of Section 3 and their accuracy. • **Measurement Validation, verification, and improvement of measure:** Sample auditing will be done • **Sequence:** 35
Metric	*Number of self-certified Section 3 businesses in HUD's registry nationwide* • **Description:** Number of self-certified Section 3 businesses in HUD's registry nationwide • **Data source:** Section 3 Business Registry System • **Unit of measurement:** Number of certified Section 3 businesses • **Dimension:** Count • **Calculation method:** Count number of businesses listed in the registry • **Frequency:** Annual • **Direction:** This is a new registry so it can only increase as more businesses are added • **Data quality (limitations/advantages of the data):** Initially there have been some problems because it was a pilot for only a few cities and businesses from other areas were registering and entering an incorrect location. • **Measurement Validation, verification, and improvement of measure** As the registry is expanded nationally, that problem will no longer continue. Early data was corrected manually. • **Sequence:** 36
Strategic Objective 3C	Promote the health and housing stability of vulnerable populations.
Metric	*Number of successful transitions through Section 811 Project Rental Assistance program* • **Description:** Number of successful PRAC 811 transitions • **Data source:** TRACS • **Unit of measurement:** Successful program transitions • **Dimension:** Count • **Calculation method:** Total number of residents of Section 811 Project Rental Assistance units • **Frequency:** Annually • **Direction:** Increase • **Data quality (limitations/advantages of the data):** TRACS will be the most current information on Section 811 PRA residents. It will provide information on previous housing settings (whether resident came from an institution, for example) and reasons for leaving the program (returning to an institution, death or other). • **Measurement Validation, verification, and improvement of measure:** Once the Section 811 PRA quarterly reporting tool is finalized and adopted, it is expected that this report will provide aggregate information about the subset of Section 811 PRA residents who came from an institution (or were at risk of moving to an institution) and the number of Section 811 PRA residents who left the program because they returned to an institution, their health status

	changed, they died, or other reason. This metric can be complemented as soon as the reporting tool is adopted. • **Sequence:** 37
Metric	*Percentage of HUD-assisted residents with public or private health coverage* • **Description:** This metric tracks the percentage of HUD-assisted residents with public or private health coverage • **Data source:** National Health Interview Survey Match to HUD tenants • **Unit of measurement:** Specified individuals with health coverage • **Dimension:** Percentage • **Calculation method:** Percent of specified individuals with health coverage divided by overall all individuals • **Frequency:** Annual • **Direction:** Increase • **Data quality (limitations/advantages of the data):** This is a rolling sample from annual surveys. Therefore the sample is not a direct, national measurement. • **Measurement Validation, verification, and improvement of measure:** NCHS experts will provide an estimate for this metric in the coming months. • **Sequence:** 38
Metric	*Number of public housing agencies with smoke-free housing policies* • **Description:** This metric tracks the percentage of public housing agencies that have public housing developments and that have adopted smoke-free housing policies • **Data source:** Published public housing agency notices, state public health agency data sources, news articles, and tracking summaries by smoking cessation groups • **Unit of measurement:** Percentage of public housing agencies with smoke-free policies • **Dimension:** Percent • **Calculation method:** Number of public housing agencies with smoke-free policies divided by number of public housing agencies with public housing developments • **Frequency:** Quarterly • **Direction:** Increased • **Data quality (limitations/advantages of the data):** Using published public housing agency notices, news articles, and tracking summaries by smoking cessation groups avoids burdening public housing agencies, but is an indirect source of data • **Measurement Validation, verification, and improvement of measure:** Reports are cross-checked for consistency re validation and verification; shifting to direct reporting by public housing agencies (into PIH's New Grants Management System, as proposed) will increase the reliability and timeliness of the data, while having a lower burden than would collecting the data separately • **Sequence:** 39
Strategic Goal 4	**Build Strong, Resilient, and Inclusive Communities**
Strategic Objective 4A	Reduce housing discrimination, affirmatively further fair housing through HUD programs, and promote diverse, inclusive communities.
Metric	*Number of people receiving remedies through Fair Housing Act enforcement work and number of people per case* • **Description:** Number of people receiving remedies and the number of people per case receiving remedies through Fair Housing Act enforcement work • **Data source:** TEAPOTS • **Unit of measurement:** Individuals and individuals per case • **Dimension:** Count and ratio • **Calculation method:** Measurement is calculated based on total of complainants, other

	aggrieved parties, additional victims receiving relief, and OGC additional victims receiving relief for HUD processed cases closed during the period that favored the complainant (conciliations, settlements, decisions in favor of the complainant, etc. i.e. with closure codes 16, 18, 30, 32, 33, 35, 37, 40, 41, 43, 50, 52, or 55). The ratio divides this number by the number of cases closed for the above mentioned reasons. • **Frequency:** Quarterly • **Direction:** The count increased from 2,043 in FY2012 to 4,147 in FY2013 and the ratio from 2.3 in FY2012 to 5.3 in FY2013 • **Data quality (limitations/advantages of the data):** The number of 'additional victims' is often an estimate so it may not be accurate. • **Measurement Validation, verification, and improvement of measure:** Under evaluation and consideration for future remedies • **Sequence:** 40
Metric	*Monetary relief per case received through Fair Housing Act enforcement work* • **Description:** Monetary relief per case through Fair Housing Act enforcement work. Cases with compensation higher than $100,000 are removed to reduce variation due to a few exceptional cases. • **Data source:** TEAPOTS • **Unit of measurement:** Dollars per case • **Dimension:** Dollars • **Calculation method:** Measurement is calculated based on total of compensation, OGC compensation, victims' fund amount, and OGC victims' fund amount less than or equal to $100,000 for HUD processed cases closed during the period that favored the complainant (conciliations, settlements, decisions in favor of the complainant, etc. i.e. with closure codes 16, 18, 30, 32, 33, 35, 37, 40, 41, 43, 50, 52, or 55) divided by the number of cases closed for the same reasons with relief less than or equal to $100,000. • **Frequency:** Quarterly • **Direction:** Increased from $2,483 in FY2012 to $3,666 in FY2013 • **Data quality (limitations/advantages of the data):** Some of the necessary fields are comparatively new to the TEAPOTS system so users may fail to complete them. Two measures are for victims' funds which are fixed dollar amounts, but it may not be certain that these amounts will be distributed. • **Measurement Validation, verification, and improvement of measure:** As users are trained to use the newer fields, the data should improve. • **Sequence:** 41
Strategic Objective 4B	Increase the health and safety of homes and embed comprehensive energy efficiency and healthy housing criteria across HUD programs.
Metric with Submetrics	*Number of HUD-assisted or –associated units completing energy efficient and healthy retrofits or new construction* • **Description:** Total number of energy efficient and healthy retrofits • **Data source:** Multiple • **Unit of measurement:** Number of energy efficient and healthy retrofits • **Dimension:** Count • **Calculation method:** Total of related-programs • **Frequency:** Varied, see submetrics below. • **Direction:** Increased • **Data quality (limitations/advantages of the data):** Varied, see submetrics below. • Measurement Validation, verification, and improvement of measure: Varied, see submetrics below. • **Sequence:** 42 Capital Fund/Indian Housing Block Grant • **Description:**

- **Data source:** PIH created the Energy and Performance Information Center (EPIC) which collects information on energy conservation measures implemented by housing authorities. Using a checklist, public housing agencies also report on all units that include 1 or more of 39 Energy Conservation Measures, as well as on new or substantial rehabilitation projects that meet ENERGY STAR for New Homes or one or more green standards.
- **Unit of measurement:** The number of specified energy retrofits
- **Dimension**: Count
- **Calculation method:** A "unit equivalent" method was developed to address these data limitations, using the top 10 most cost-effective measures.
- **Frequency:** Quarterly
- **Direction:** Increased
- **Data quality (limitations/advantages of the data):** The energy data collected is self-reported and limited; each Energy Conservation Measure is reported separately for each unit (by project) but not bundles so as to report on which bundle of Energy Conservation Measures was installed in a particular unit. Other data limitations are that HUD does not collect pre- and post-retrofit consumption data for these measures, or Energy Conservation Measure costs, so determinations of cost effectiveness for these investments must be estimates, using recognized engineering or costs methods.
- **Measurement Validation, verification, and improvement of measure:** Public and Indian Housing staff validates the data entered into the system in terms of completeness of information. Public and Indian Housing staff provides information to grantees to ensure that the definitional boundaries of data prompts are fully understood. Data may also be confirmed through remote and onsite reviews of public housing agencies.
- **Sequence:** 42a

Energy Performance Contracts (EPC)
- **Description:**
- **Data source:** The data used for reporting for the Energy Performance Contract program were gathered through the Energy Performance Contract Inventory, which all Public and Indian Housing field offices are required to complete annually.
- **Unit of measurement:** Number of Energy Performance Contract Units with Retrofits
- **Dimension**: Count
- **Calculation method:** Every unit incorporated into EPC
- **Frequency:** Annually
- **Direction:** Increased
- **Data quality (limitations/advantages of the data):** For the first time, in FY 2010, the Energy Performance Contract Inventory was restructured to gather data at the asset management project level rather than at the contract level. Training was provided to the field offices to increase the reporting accuracy and completeness. Despite this effort, the Energy Performance Contract Inventory frequently contains missing or erroneous data.
- **Measurement Validation, verification, and improvement of measure:** The data are reviewed for suspected inaccuracies. When reporting data, the Office of Public and Indian Housing makes a strong effort to confirm the data are valid and makes corrections as noted. The Office of Public and Indian Housing is endeavoring to improve the Energy Performance Contract Inventory to make it easier to complete, thus improving accuracy and completeness. At the same time, the Office of Public and Indian Housing is working to integrate the Energy Performance Contract Inventory with its existing reporting systems, which tend to be more sophisticated, yet easier to use.
- **Sequence:** 42b

Developed Energy Efficient Units (HOPE VI/Mixed-Finance/Choice Neighborhoods)
- **Description:** Developed Energy Efficient Units
- **Data source:** The HOPE VI Grants Management System

- **Unit of measurement:** Units built to green standard
- **Dimension:** Count
- **Calculation method:** Units built to green standard
- **Frequency:** Quarterly
- **Direction:** Increased
- **Data quality (limitations/advantages of the data):** For the first time, during FY 2010, the Grants Management System was expanded to collect information on whether the HOPE VI units being built were achieving a comprehensive green standard (for example, LEED for Homes), a non-comprehensive energy-efficiency standard (for example, ENERGY STAR for New Homes), or meeting the local building code. The Grants Management System has some limitations. In particular, the data are self-reported. The data collected through the system are limited in scope to the achievement of green standards. Although these standards are the highest ideal, no data are collected about building practices that are better than the minimum, but yet, the practices do not reach the level of a green standard.
- **Measurement Validation, verification, and improvement of measure:** Grantees are required to use the data system quarterly. Each quarter, the grants manager in charge of each project checks the data for reasonableness. In addition, the HOPE VI program has a data collection contractor on staff to provide technical assistance to grantees that are completing their reporting requirements.
- **Sequence:** 42c

Better Buildings – PIH
- **Description:** To make PIH buildings 20% more energy efficient over the next 10 years and accelerate private sector investment in energy efficiency.
- **Data source: Data collection mechanism under development**
- **Unit of measurement: See above**
- **Dimension: See above**
- **Calculation method: See above**
- **Frequency: See above**
- **Direction: Increase**
- **Data quality (limitations/advantages of the data): See above**
- **Measurement Validation, verification, and improvement of measure: See above**
- **Sequence: 42e**

Community Planning Development
Home Investment Partnerships
- **Description:**
- **Data source:** IDIS
- **Unit of measurement:** Housing units
- **Dimension:** Count
- **Calculation method:** Data is derived from grantee accomplishments reported by CDBG grantees in the Integrated Disbursement and Information System.
- **Frequency:** Quarterly
- **Direction:** Increased
- **Data quality (limitations/advantages of the data):** Data reliability has been enhanced by the re-engineering of the system at the end of FY 2009 into FY 2010.
- **Measurement Validation, verification, and improvement of measure:** When monitoring grantees, Community Planning and Development field staff verifies program data.
- **Sequence:** 42f

CDBG—Energy Star

- **Description**: The number of newly constructed units in the CDBG program which have been identified by grantees as Energy Star
- **Data source**: Aggregated (summed) raw data on accomplishments reported by Community Development Block Grant grantees in the Integrated Disbursement and Information System.
- **Unit of measurement**: Housing Units
- **Dimension**: Count
- **Calculation method**: Data is derived from grantee accomplishments reported by CDBG grantees in the Integrated Disbursement and Information System.
- **Frequency**: Quarterly
- **Direction**:Increased
- **Data quality (limitations/advantages of the data)**: Data reliability has been enhanced by the re-engineering of the system at the end of FY 2009 into FY 2010.
- **Measurement Validation, verification, and improvement of measure**: When monitoring grantees, Community Planning and Development field staff verifies program data.
- **Sequence**: 42g

CDBG-DR Sandy—Green
- **Description:** The number of new construction units and substantially rehabilitated units (including reconstruction) funded by the CDBG-DR Sandy allocation. All of these types of units are required to meet one of the green building certification standards identified by Notice.
- **Data source:** DRGR
- **Unit of measurement:** Number of substantially rehabilitated units
- **Dimension:** Count
- **Calculation method:** Data is derived from CDBG-DR Sandy grantee projections reported in DRGR.
- **Frequency: Quarterly**
- **Direction: Increase**
- **Data quality (limitations/advantages of the data):** Sandy grantees are still providing projections
- **Measurement Validation, verification, and improvement of measure:** Sandy grantees are still providing projections
- **Sequence**: 42h

Multifamily

MF Endorsements
- **Description:** Finally endorsed FHA-insured units that are retrofitted with energy efficient features
- **Data source:** DAP and SharePoint site for MAP goals for insured production as reported for MAP goal 4C
- **Unit of measurement:** Number of units
- **Dimension:** Count
- **Calculation method:** Total count of finally endorsed FHA-insured units that are retrofitted with energy efficient features
- **Frequency:** Monthly
- **Direction:** Increasing
- **Data quality (limitations/advantages of the data):** Newly constructed or substantially rehabilitated properties with tax credits or tax-exempt bond financing are tracked in DAP. Other properties with certified green design. Energy Star appliances, Energy Star systems, or Water Sense must be entered post-endorsement into a SharePoint site developed specifically to track this goal. Since the site is updated independently of DAP, there is no assurance that

all applicable units are reported in SharePoint.

- **Measurement Validation, verification, and improvement of measure:** The purpose of a loan (for example, new construction, substantial rehabilitation) and special characteristics (for example, LIHTC, tax exempt bonds) which were entered in DAP by technical staff in insured production are displayed on DAP Form HUD-290 which is reviewed and signed by Hub and Program Center Directors and so are considered to be reliable.
- **Sequence:** 42l

Mark to Market

- **Description:** The Rehabilitation Escrow Administration database, a system maintained to track and approve retrofit schedules, costs, and specifications, and used to review and approve funding draws on completion and verification of work completion.
- **Data source:** OAHP data system as reported for MAP goal 4A
- **Unit of measurement:** The number of units retrofitted with energy efficient features through the Mark to Market program
- **Dimension:** Count
- **Calculation method:** Total number of units retrofitted with energy efficient features through the Mark to Market program
- **Frequency:** Monthly
- **Direction:** Increasing
- **Data quality (limitations/advantages of the data):** The Agency has a high degree of confidence in the accuracy of the data. Basic transaction parameters are derived from official record sources—Mark-to-Market system and Rehabilitation Escrow Administrations database—and locked down in the independently maintained database.
- **Measurement Validation, verification, and improvement of measure:** Limited and finite number of properties being tracked; independently maintained database; accessible only by a limited number of highly trained professionals, minimizing the opportunity for user input errors or data corruption; regular reports from the database allow for a reality check period over period; Approved Funds Control Plans and Front End Risk Assessments require a high degree of review and approval for accuracy (that is, the process ensures quality data).
- **Sequence:** 42m

Section 202/811

- **Description:** The number of units retrofitted with energy efficient features through the 202/811 program
- **Data source:** Multifamily Portfolio Reporting Database (MPRD) as reported for MAP goal 4B
- **Unit of measurement:** Number of units retrofitted with energy efficient features
- **Dimension:** Count
- **Calculation method:** Total number of units retrofitted with energy efficient features through the 202/811 program
- **Frequency:** Monthly
- **Direction:** Increasing
- **Data quality (limitations/advantages of the data):** 202/811 program data is drawn from the Multifamily Portfolio Reporting Database which is populated by the integrated Real Estate Management System (iREMS). iREMS is the official source of data on Multifamily Housing's portfolio of insured and assisted properties. iREMS obtains its data from interfacing systems as well as user entry. iREMS uses the HEREMS database, which serves as Housing's and DEC's centralized database. For 202/811 development purposes HEREMS obtains its data from the Development Application Processing (DAP) system.
- **Measurement Validation, verification, and improvement of measure:** The activity indicator used to calculate the 202/811 energy efficiency measure is "dap_construction_completion_dt". The energy efficiency requirement was incentivized in the FY2009 NOFA selection process and was mandated in the FY 2010 NOFA. Therefore every 202/811 project funded in FY 2010 and virtually every one funded in FY 2009 that have completed construction count towards the

goal. Thus, the information is considered to valid and reliable.

- **Sequence: 42n**

Green Refi Plus

- **Description:** The number of QPE green risk sharing applications that have been finally endorsed.
- **Data source:** DAP
- **Unit of measurement:** The number of applications that have been finally endorsed.
- **Dimension: Count**
- **Calculation method:** Total count of applications under the QPE risk sharing program that have been finally endorsed
- **Frequency:** Quarterly
- **Direction:** Increasing
- **Data quality (limitations/advantages of the data):** The Agency has a high degree of confidence in the accuracy of the data that has been entered in DAP.
- **Measurement Validation, verification, and improvement of measure:** The purpose of a loan (for example, refinancing) and the section of the act (which identifies risk sharing) which were entered in DAP by technical staff in insured production are displayed on DAP Form HUD-290 which is reviewed and signed by Hub and Program Center Directors and so are considered to be reliable.
- **Sequence:** 42p

Better Buildings – MF

- **Description:** The number of partners that are participating in the Better Building Challenge (BBC)
- **Data source:** BBC tracking database
- **Unit of measurement:** The number of partners that are participating in the Better Building Challenge
- **Dimension:** Count
- **Calculation method:** Total count of partners that are participating in the Better Building Challenge
- **Frequency:** Monthly
- **Direction:** Increasing
- **Data quality (limitations/advantages of the data):** Data on partner names comes from report provided by a consultant to HUD MF BBC Lead Kevin Bush, in OER. Mara Blitzer adds the other information – HQ location, hub office location, and region associated – that she collects herself into the tracking database that is attached to the MAP report.
- **Measurement Validation, verification, and improvement of measure:** Hub office staff review the tracking database to see whether a partner entity is missing or if the entity has been incorrectly assigned to the hub office or region. We don't have a protocol in place for improving the measure.
- **Sequence:** 42q

Single Family
EEMs

- **Description:** Total number of Energy Efficient Mortgages
- **Data source:** Single Family Data Warehouse
- **Unit of measurement:** Number of Energy Efficient Mortgages
- **Dimension:** Count
- **Calculation method:** Excel Count
- **Frequency:** Quarterly
- **Direction:** Reduction of trending decline

- **Data quality (limitations/advantages of the data):** Dependent on lender's input of info.
- **Measurement Validation, verification, and improvement of measure:** None
- **Sequence:** 42m

PowerSaver (Title 1)
- **Description:** Total number of PowerSaver loans
- **Data source:** Single Family Data Warehouse
- **Unit of measurement:** Number of PowerSaver Title I loans
- **Dimension:** Count
- **Calculation method:** Excel Count
- **Frequency:** Quarterly
- **Direction:** Stable
- **Data quality (limitations/advantages of the data):** Lender supplied is good as reporting is connected to grant funds.
- **Measurement Validation, verification, and improvement of measure:** None
- **Sequence:** 42n

203K
- **Description:** Total number of PowerSaver 203(k) loans
- **Data source:** Single Family Data Warehouse
- **Unit of measurement:** Number of PowerSaver loans
- **Dimension:** Count
- **Calculation method:** Excel Count
- **Frequency:** Quarterly
- **Direction:** Stable
- **Data quality (limitations/advantages of the data):** Lender supplied is good as reporting is connected to grant funds.
- **Sequence:** 42o

Office of Healthy Homes and Lead Hazard Control
Lead Hazard Control
- **Description:** Number of housing units made lead-safe through lead hazard control grants
- **Data source:** Grantee reports to Healthy Homes Grant Management System
- **Unit of measurement:** Housing units
- **Dimension:** Count
- **Calculation method:** Total of units from each grantee
- **Frequency:** Quarterly
- **Direction:** Increased
- **Data quality (limitations/advantages of the data):** Units are counted only after payment has been made after lead hazard control work has been done and the units have been cleared for re-occupancy, so grantees have a fiduciary responsibility to report accurately; but some grantees report on a single unit more than once, as they make partial and then final payments
- **Measurement Validation, verification, and improvement of measure:** Reports are validated against financial payments (LOCCS reporting), and verified by remote and on-site monitoring by grant Government Technical Representatives. Having software checks for duplicate counting of units would improve the measure.
- **Sequence:** 42p

Healthy Homes
- **Description:** Number of housing units made healthier and/or safer through healthy homes grants
- **Data source:** Grantee reports to Healthy Homes Grant Management System

- **Unit of measurement:** Housing units
- **Dimension:** Count
- **Calculation method:** Total of units from each grantee
- **Frequency:** Quarterly
- **Direction:** Increased
- **Data quality (limitations/advantages of the data):** Units are counted only after payment has been made after hazard control work has been done and re-occupancy has been allowed, so grantees have a fiduciary responsibility to report accurately; but some grantees report on a single unit more than once, as they make partial and then final payments
- **Measurement Validation, verification, and improvement of measure:** Reports are validated against financial payments (LOCCS reporting), and verified by remote and on-site monitoring by grant Government Technical Representatives. Having software checks for duplicate counting of units would improve the measure.
- **Sequence:** 42q

Lead Hazard Enforcement
- **Description:** Housing units made lead-safe per agreements or orders under the Lead Disclosure Rule
- **Data source:** Property owner/property manager reports
- **Unit of measurement:** Housing units
- **Dimension:** Count
- **Calculation method:** Total of units from each owner/manager
- **Frequency:** Quarterly
- **Direction:** Increased
- **Data quality (limitations/advantages of the data):** Units are counted only after the owners/managers have documented completing work and the units have been tested and for low lead levels that would allow re-occupancy, so owners/managers face economic and/or court sanctions for not reporting accurately; but limitations on HUD staffing and travel funding preclude on-site quality control checking.
- **Measurement Validation, verification, and improvement of measure:** Lead hazard control work is validated by consistency checks on records from owners/managers, and verified by EPA- or State-certified lead risk assessors; measure could be improved with routine on-site quality control checking by HUD lead program enforcement and/or its lead enforcement partners.
- **Sequence:** 42r

Lead Safe Housing Rule - HOME-CDBG-HOPWA
- **Description:** Housing units made lead safe through work under HUD's Lead Safe Housing Rule
- **Data source:** Reporting by funding recipients as tracked by CPD's Integrated Disbursement and Information System (IDIS)
- **Unit of measurement:** Housing units
- **Dimension:** Count
- **Calculation method:** Total of units from each funding recipient
- **Frequency:** Quarterly
- **Direction:** Increased
- **Data quality (limitations/advantages of the data):** Units are counted only after payment has been made for completing work and allowing re-occupancy, so funding recipients have a fiduciary responsibility to report accurately; routine on-site quality control checking for lead results by HUD lead program enforcement and/or its lead enforcement partners is not conducted.
- **Measurement Validation, verification, and improvement of measure:** Reports are validated against financial payments (LOCCS reporting), and verified by remote and on-site

	monitoring by CPD representatives. Measure would be improved by routine on-site quality control checking for lead results by HUD lead program enforcement and/or its lead enforcement partners. • **Sequence:** 42s
Strategic Objective 4C	Support the recovery of communities from disasters by promoting community resilience, developing state and local capacity, and ensuring a coordinated federal response that reduces risk and produces a more resilient built environment.
Metric	*Percentage of Sandy Task Force recommendations related to disaster recovery and resilience that have been completed* • **Description:** Percentage of Sandy Task Force recommendations related to disaster recovery and resilience that have been completed • **Data source:** Sandy PMO • **Unit of measurement:** Percentage of completed recommendations for disaster recovery • **Dimension:** Percentage • **Calculation method:** Completed recommendations divided by total recommendations • **Frequency:** Quarterly • **Direction:** Increase • **Data quality (limitations/advantages of the data):** Recommendation completion is determined and reported by individual agencies that own each recommendation. Targets for this metric are based on agency projections for completion but changing circumstances can alter the work plans for each recommendation and thus the timeframe for completion of the measure. • **Measurement Validation, verification, and improvement of measure:** Recommendation completion is determined and reported by individual agencies that own each recommendation. Targets for this metric are based on agency projections for completion but changing circumstances can alter the work plans for each recommendation and thus the timeframe for completion of the measure. • **Sequence:** 43
Strategic Objective 4D	Strengthen communities' economic health, resilience and access to opportunity.
	HUD is developing metrics to track progress on this objective. Metrics will be provided in our annual amendment to the Strategic Plan.